ISBN 0-8373-0701-0

C-701   CAREER EXAMINATION SERIES

This is your
PASSBOOK® for.

School Custodian-Engineer

Test Preparation Study Guide

Questions & Answers

NLC

NATIONAL LEARNING CORPORATION

PASSBOOK®

NOTICE

This book is SOLELY intended for, is sold ONLY to, and its use is RESTRICTED to *individual*, bona fide applicants or candidates who qualify by virtue of having seriously filed applications for appropriate license, certificate, professional and/or promotional advancement, higher school matriculation, scholarship, or other legitimate requirements of educational and/or governmental authorities.

This book is NOT intended for use, class instruction, tutoring, training, duplication, copying, reprinting, excerption, or adaptation, etc., by:

(1) Other publishers

(2) Proprietors and/or Instructors of "Coaching" and/or Preparatory Courses

(3) Personnel and/or Training Divisions of commercial, industrial, and governmental organizations

(4) Schools, colleges, or universities and/or their departments and staffs, including teachers and other personnel

(5) Testing Agencies or Bureaus

(6) Study groups which seek by the purchase of a single volume to copy and/or duplicate and/or adapt this material for use by the group as a whole without having purchased individual volumes for each of the members of the group

(7) Et al.

Such persons would be in violation of appropriate Federal and State statutes.

PROVISION OF LICENSING AGREEMENTS. — Recognized educational commercial, industrial, and governmental institutions and organizations, and others legitimately engaged in educational pursuits, including training, testing, and measurement activities, may address a request for a licensing agreement to the copyright owners, who will determine whether, and under what conditions, including fees and charges, the materials in this book may be used by them. In other words, a licensing facility exists for the legitimate use of the material in this book on other than an individual basis. However, it is asseverated and affirmed here that the material in this book *CANNOT* be used without the receipt of the express permission of such a licensing agreement from the Publishers.

NATIONAL LEARNING CORPORATION
212 Michael Drive
Syosset, New York 11791

Inquiries re licensing agreements should be addressed to:
The President
National Learning Corporation
212 Michael Drive
Syosset, New York 11791

PASSBOOK® SERIES

THE *PASSBOOK® SERIES* has been created to prepare applicants and candidates for the ultimate academic battlefield — the examination room.

At some time in our lives, each and every one of us may be required to take an examination — for validation, matriculation, admission, qualification, registration, certification, or licensure.

Based on the assumption that every applicant or candidate has met the basic formal educational standards, has taken the required number of courses, and read the necessary texts, the *PASSBOOK® SERIES* furnishes the one special preparation which may assure passing with confidence, instead of failing with insecurity. Examination questions — together with answers — are furnished as the basic vehicle for study so that the mysteries of the examination and its compounding difficulties may be eliminated or diminished by a sure method.

This book is meant to help you pass your examination provided that you qualify and are serious in your objective.

The entire field is reviewed through the huge store of content information which is succinctly presented through a provocative and challenging approach — the question-and-answer method.

A climate of success is established by furnishing the correct answers at the end of each test.

You soon learn to recognize types of questions, forms of questions, and patterns of questioning. You may even begin to anticipate expected outcomes.

You perceive that many questions are repeated or adapted so that you can gain acute insights, which may enable you to score many sure points.

You learn how to confront new questions, or types of questions, and to attack them confidently and work out the correct answers.

You note objectives and emphases, and recognize pitfalls and dangers, so that you may make positive educational adjustments.

Moreover, you are kept fully informed in relation to new concepts, methods, practices, and directions in the field.

You discover that you are actually taking the examination all the time: you are preparing for the examination by "taking" an examination, not by reading extraneous and/or supererogatory textbooks.

In short, this PASSBOOK®, used directedly, should be an important factor in helping you to pass your test.

SCHOOL CUSTODIAN-ENGINEER

JOB DESCRIPTION

Under general supervision, supervises a custodial maintenance staff and is responsible for the physical operation, maintenance, repair, and custodial upkeep and care of a public school building and its immediate grounds; performs related work.

EXAMPLES OF TYPICAL TASKS

Operates and is responsible for all electrical and mechanical equipment including air conditioning, heating, ventilation, refrigeration, water supply and sewage systems, electric elevators and elevator equipment, automatic signal systems, electrical generating plants, filtration plants, and cleaning equipment. Makes minor repairs. Supervises cleaning of buildings and grounds. Conducts inspection of building to determine needed repairs. Consults with and advises officials on problems of operation, maintenance and repairs. Sets up the work schedules to insure maximum efficiency and minimum interference with classroom activities. Requisitions and accounts for custodial and maintenance materials, tools and supplies. Maintains records and prepares required reports of plant operations. Hires and trains personnel. Is responsible for his or her personnel's payroll and forms; pays wages; deducts payroll taxes, state disability insurance, court ordered garnishees and union dues. Provides for workers' compensation insurance.

TEST DESCRIPTION

The multiple-choice test may include questions in the following areas: procedures for operation and maintenance of boiler systems; procedures for operation and maintenance of HVAC systems; procedures for operation and maintenance of fire protection and life safety systems; procedures for troubleshooting heating, ventilation, plumbing, electrical, carpentry, and lighting problems; procedures for replacement, repair, and maintenance of components of plumbing and electrical systems; procedures for maintenance of building exterior and surrounding grounds; procedures for repair of walls, floors, windows, doors, and other building structures and replacement of component parts (e.g., tiles, panes, hinges, locks), including related carpentry and use of fasteners; procedures for operation and maintenance of water supply and drainage systems; painting and finishing procedures and use of related materials; cleaning procedures for all areas of the building and use of cleaning products; safety procedures and use of personal protective equipment related to all custodial operations; purposes, use, and maintenance of hand tools, electrical tools, and gas-powered equipment; financial principles and their application to management of budgets, including cash flow management and bookkeeping; mathematical principles and their application to performance of job duties, including arithmetic calculations (using whole numbers, fractions, and decimals), ratios, percentages, and job-relevant formulas; written communication, including the ability to read and understand information and ideas presented in writing and to communicate information and ideas in writing so others will understand; and other related areas.

HOW TO TAKE A TEST

I. YOU MUST PASS AN EXAMINATION

A. *WHAT EVERY CANDIDATE SHOULD KNOW*

Examination applicants often ask us for help in preparing for the written test. What can I study in advance? What kinds of questions will be asked? How will the test be given? How will the papers be graded?

As an applicant for a civil service examination, you may be wondering about some of these things. Our purpose here is to suggest effective methods of advance study and to describe civil service examinations.

Your chances for success on this examination can be increased if you know how to prepare. Those "pre-examination jitters" can be reduced if you know what to expect. You can even experience an adventure in good citizenship if you know why civil service exams are given.

B. *WHY ARE CIVIL SERVICE EXAMINATIONS GIVEN?*

Civil service examinations are important to you in two ways. As a citizen, you want public jobs filled by employees who know how to do their work. As a job seeker, you want a fair chance to compete for that job on an equal footing with other candidates. The best-known means of accomplishing this two-fold goal is the competitive examination.

Exams are widely publicized throughout the nation. They may be administered for jobs in federal, state, city, municipal, town or village governments or agencies.

Any citizen may apply, with some limitations, such as the age or residence of applicants. Your experience and education may be reviewed to see whether you meet the requirements for the particular examination. When these requirements exist, they are reasonable and applied consistently to all applicants. Thus, a competitive examination may cause you some uneasiness now, but it is your privilege and safeguard.

C. *HOW ARE CIVIL SERVICE EXAMS DEVELOPED?*

Examinations are carefully written by trained technicians who are specialists in the field known as "psychological measurement," in consultation with recognized authorities in the field of work that the test will cover. These experts recommend the subject matter areas or skills to be tested; only those knowledges or skills important to your success on the job are included. The most reliable books and source materials available are used as references. Together, the experts and technicians judge the difficulty level of the questions.

Test technicians know how to phrase questions so that the problem is clearly stated. Their ethics do not permit "trick" or "catch" questions. Questions may have been tried out on sample groups, or subjected to statistical analysis, to determine their usefulness.

Written tests are often used in combination with performance tests, ratings of training and experience, and oral interviews. All of these measures combine to form the best-known means of finding the right person for the right job.

II. HOW TO PASS THE WRITTEN TEST

A. NATURE OF THE EXAMINATION

To prepare intelligently for civil service examinations, you should know how they differ from school examinations you have taken. In school you were assigned certain definite pages to read or subjects to cover. The examination questions were quite detailed and usually emphasized memory. Civil service exams, on the other hand, try to discover your present ability to perform the duties of a position, plus your potentiality to learn these duties. In other words, a civil service exam attempts to predict how successful you will be. Questions cover such a broad area that they cannot be as minute and detailed as school exam questions.

In the public service similar kinds of work, or positions, are grouped together in one "class." This process is known as *position-classification*. All the positions in a class are paid according to the salary range for that class. One class title covers all of these positions, and they are all tested by the same examination.

B. FOUR BASIC STEPS

1) Study the announcement

How, then, can you know what subjects to study? Our best answer is: "Learn as much as possible about the class of positions for which you've applied." The exam will test the knowledge, skills and abilities needed to do the work.

Your most valuable source of information about the position you want is the official exam announcement. This announcement lists the training and experience qualifications. Check these standards and apply only if you come reasonably close to meeting them.

The brief description of the position in the examination announcement offers some clues to the subjects which will be tested. Think about the job itself. Review the duties in your mind. Can you perform them, or are there some in which you are rusty? Fill in the blank spots in your preparation.

Many jurisdictions preview the written test in the exam announcement by including a section called "Knowledge and Abilities Required," "Scope of the Examination," or some similar heading. Here you will find out specifically what fields will be tested.

2) Review your own background

Once you learn in general what the position is all about, and what you need to know to do the work, ask yourself which subjects you already know fairly well and which need improvement. You may wonder whether to concentrate on improving your strong areas or on building some background in your fields of weakness. When the announcement has specified "some knowledge" or "considerable knowledge," or has used adjectives like "beginning principles of..." or "advanced ... methods," you can get a clue as to the number and difficulty of questions to be asked in any given field. More questions, and hence broader coverage, would be included for those subjects which are more important in the work. Now weigh your strengths and weaknesses against the job requirements and prepare accordingly.

3) Determine the level of the position

Another way to tell how intensively you should prepare is to understand the level of the job for which you are applying. Is it the entering level? In other words, is this the position in which beginners in a field of work are hired? Or is it an intermediate or advanced level? Sometimes this is indicated by such words as "Junior" or "Senior" in the class title. Other jurisdictions use Roman numerals to designate the level – Clerk I, Clerk II, for example. The word "Supervisor" sometimes appears in the title. If the level is not indicated by the title, check the description of duties. Will you be working under very close supervision, or will you have responsibility for independent decisions in this work?

4) Choose appropriate study materials

Now that you know the subjects to be examined and the relative amount of each subject to be covered, you can choose suitable study materials. For beginning level jobs, or even advanced ones, if you have a pronounced weakness in some aspect of your training, read a modern, standard textbook in that field. Be sure it is up to date and has general coverage. Such books are normally available at your library, and the librarian will be glad to help you locate one. For entry-level positions, questions of appropriate difficulty are chosen – neither highly advanced questions, nor those too simple. Such questions require careful thought but not advanced training.

If the position for which you are applying is technical or advanced, you will read more advanced, specialized material. If you are already familiar with the basic principles of your field, elementary textbooks would waste your time. Concentrate on advanced textbooks and technical periodicals. Think through the concepts and review difficult problems in your field.

These are all general sources. You can get more ideas on your own initiative, following these leads. For example, training manuals and publications of the government agency which employs workers in your field can be useful, particularly for technical and professional positions. A letter or visit to the government department involved may result in more specific study suggestions, and certainly will provide you with a more definite idea of the exact nature of the position you are seeking.

III. KINDS OF TESTS

Tests are used for purposes other than measuring knowledge and ability to perform specified duties. For some positions, it is equally important to test ability to make adjustments to new situations or to profit from training. In others, basic mental abilities not dependent on information are essential. Questions which test these things may not appear as pertinent to the duties of the position as those which test for knowledge and information. Yet they are often highly important parts of a fair examination. For very general questions, it is almost impossible to help you direct your study efforts. What we can do is to point out some of the more common of these general abilities needed in public service positions and describe some typical questions.

1) General information

Broad, general information has been found useful for predicting job success in some kinds of work. This is tested in a variety of ways, from vocabulary lists to questions about current events. Basic background in some field of work, such as sociology or economics, may be sampled in a group of questions. Often these are principles which have become familiar to most persons through exposure rather than through formal training. It is difficult to advise you how to study for these questions; being alert to the world around you is our best suggestion.

2) Verbal ability

An example of an ability needed in many positions is verbal or language ability. Verbal ability is, in brief, the ability to use and understand words. Vocabulary and grammar tests are typical measures of this ability. Reading comprehension or paragraph interpretation questions are common in many kinds of civil service tests. You are given a paragraph of written material and asked to find its central meaning.

3) Numerical ability

Number skills can be tested by the familiar arithmetic problem, by checking paired lists of numbers to see which are alike and which are different, or by interpreting charts and graphs. In the latter test, a graph may be printed in the test booklet which you are asked to use as the basis for answering questions.

4) Observation

A popular test for law-enforcement positions is the observation test. A picture is shown to you for several minutes, then taken away. Questions about the picture test your ability to observe both details and larger elements.

5) Following directions

In many positions in the public service, the employee must be able to carry out written instructions dependably and accurately. You may be given a chart with several columns, each column listing a variety of information. The questions require you to carry out directions involving the information given in the chart.

6) Skills and aptitudes

Performance tests effectively measure some manual skills and aptitudes. When the skill is one in which you are trained, such as typing or shorthand, you can practice. These tests are often very much like those given in business school or high school courses. For many of the other skills and aptitudes, however, no short-time preparation can be made. Skills and abilities natural to you or that you have developed throughout your lifetime are being tested.

Many of the general questions just described provide all the data needed to answer the questions and ask you to use your reasoning ability to find the answers. Your best preparation for these tests, as well as for tests of facts and ideas, is to be at your physical and mental best. You, no doubt, have your own methods of getting into an exam-taking mood and keeping "in shape." The next section lists some ideas on this subject.

IV. KINDS OF QUESTIONS

Only rarely is the "essay" question, which you answer in narrative form, used in civil service tests. Civil service tests are usually of the short-answer type. Full instructions for answering these questions will be given to you at the examination. But in case this is your first experience with short-answer questions and separate answer sheets, here is what you need to know:

1) Multiple-choice Questions

Most popular of the short-answer questions is the "multiple choice" or "best answer" question. It can be used, for example, to test for factual knowledge, ability to solve problems or judgment in meeting situations found at work.

A multiple-choice question is normally one of three types—

- It can begin with an incomplete statement followed by several possible endings. You are to find the one ending which *best* completes the statement, although some of the others may not be entirely wrong.
- It can also be a complete statement in the form of a question which is answered by choosing one of the statements listed.
- It can be in the form of a problem – again you select the best answer.

Here is an example of a multiple-choice question with a discussion which should give you some clues as to the method for choosing the right answer:

When an employee has a complaint about his assignment, the action which will *best* help him overcome his difficulty is to
- A. discuss his difficulty with his coworkers
- B. take the problem to the head of the organization
- C. take the problem to the person who gave him the assignment
- D. say nothing to anyone about his complaint

In answering this question, you should study each of the choices to find which is best. Consider choice "A" – Certainly an employee may discuss his complaint with fellow employees, but no change or improvement can result, and the complaint remains unresolved. Choice "B" is a poor choice since the head of the organization probably does not know what assignment you have been given, and taking your problem to him is known as "going over the head" of the supervisor. The supervisor, or person who made the assignment, is the person who can clarify it or correct any injustice. Choice "C" is, therefore, correct. To say nothing, as in choice "D," is unwise. Supervisors have and interest in knowing the problems employees are facing, and the employee is seeking a solution to his problem.

2) True/False Questions

The "true/false" or "right/wrong" form of question is sometimes used. Here a complete statement is given. Your job is to decide whether the statement is right or wrong.

SAMPLE: A person-to-person long-distance telephone call costs less than a station-to-station call to the same city.

This statement is wrong, or false, since person-to-person calls are more expensive.

This is not a complete list of all possible question forms, although most of the others are variations of these common types. You will always get complete directions for answering questions. Be sure you understand *how* to mark your answers – ask questions until you do.

V. RECORDING YOUR ANSWERS

For an examination with very few applicants, you may be told to record your answers in the test booklet itself. Separate answer sheets are much more common. If this separate answer sheet is to be scored by machine – and this is often the case – it is highly important that you mark your answers correctly in order to get credit.

An electric scoring machine is often used in civil service offices because of the speed with which papers can be scored. Machine-scored answer sheets must be marked with a pencil, which will be given to you. This pencil has a high graphite content which responds to the electric scoring machine. As a matter of fact, stray dots may register as answers, so do not let your pencil rest on the answer sheet while you are pondering the correct answer. Also, if your pencil lead breaks or is otherwise defective, ask for another.

Since the answer sheet will be dropped in a slot in the scoring machine, be careful not to bend the corners or get the paper crumpled.

The answer sheet normally has five vertical columns of numbers, with 30 numbers to a column. These numbers correspond to the question numbers in your test booklet. After each number, going across the page are four or five pairs of dotted lines. These short dotted lines have small letters or numbers above them. The first two pairs may also have a "T" or "F" above the letters. This indicates that the first two pairs only are to be used if the questions are of the true-false type. If the questions are multiple choice, disregard the "T" and "F" and pay attention only to the small letters or numbers.

Answer your questions in the manner of the sample that follows:

32. The largest city in the United States is
    A. Washington, D.C.
    B. New York City
    C. Chicago
    D. Detroit
    E. San Francisco

1) Choose the answer you think is best. (New York City is the largest, so "B" is correct.)
2) Find the row of dotted lines numbered the same as the question you are answering. (Find row number 32)
3) Find the pair of dotted lines corresponding to the answer. (Find the pair of lines under the mark "B.")
4) Make a solid black mark between the dotted lines.

VI. BEFORE THE TEST

Common sense will help you find procedures to follow to get ready for an examination. Too many of us, however, overlook these sensible measures. Indeed, nervousness and fatigue have been found to be the most serious reasons why applicants fail to do their best on civil service tests. Here is a list of reminders:

- Begin your preparation early – Don't wait until the last minute to go scurrying around for books and materials or to find out what the position is all about.
- Prepare continuously – An hour a night for a week is better than an all-night cram session. This has been definitely established. What is more, a night a

week for a month will return better dividends than crowding your study into a shorter period of time.

- Locate the place of the exam – You have been sent a notice telling you when and where to report for the examination. If the location is in a different town or otherwise unfamiliar to you, it would be well to inquire the best route and learn something about the building.
- Relax the night before the test – Allow your mind to rest. Do not study at all that night. Plan some mild recreation or diversion; then go to bed early and get a good night's sleep.
- Get up early enough to make a leisurely trip to the place for the test – This way unforeseen events, traffic snarls, unfamiliar buildings, etc. will not upset you.
- Dress comfortably – A written test is not a fashion show. You will be known by number and not by name, so wear something comfortable.
- Leave excess paraphernalia at home – Shopping bags and odd bundles will get in your way. You need bring only the items mentioned in the official notice you received; usually everything you need is provided. Do not bring reference books to the exam. They will only confuse those last minutes and be taken away from you when in the test room.
- Arrive somewhat ahead of time – If because of transportation schedules you must get there very early, bring a newspaper or magazine to take your mind off yourself while waiting.
- Locate the examination room – When you have found the proper room, you will be directed to the seat or part of the room where you will sit. Sometimes you are given a sheet of instructions to read while you are waiting. Do not fill out any forms until you are told to do so; just read them and be prepared.
- Relax and prepare to listen to the instructions
- If you have any physical problem that may keep you from doing your best, be sure to tell the test administrator. If you are sick or in poor health, you really cannot do your best on the exam. You can come back and take the test some other time.

VII. AT THE TEST

The day of the test is here and you have the test booklet in your hand. The temptation to get going is very strong. Caution! There is more to success than knowing the right answers. You must know how to identify your papers and understand variations in the type of short-answer question used in this particular examination. Follow these suggestions for maximum results from your efforts:

1) Cooperate with the monitor
The test administrator has a duty to create a situation in which you can be as much at ease as possible. He will give instructions, tell you when to begin, check to see that you are marking your answer sheet correctly, and so on. He is not there to guard you, although he will see that your competitors do not take unfair advantage. He wants to help you do your best.

2) Listen to all instructions
Don't jump the gun! Wait until you understand all directions. In most civil service tests you get more time than you need to answer the questions. So don't be in a hurry.

Read each word of instructions until you clearly understand the meaning. Study the examples, listen to all announcements and follow directions. Ask questions if you do not understand what to do.

3) Identify your papers

Civil service exams are usually identified by number only. You will be assigned a number; you must not put your name on your test papers. Be sure to copy your number correctly. Since more than one exam may be given, copy your exact examination title.

4) Plan your time

Unless you are told that a test is a "speed" or "rate of work" test, speed itself is usually not important. Time enough to answer all the questions will be provided, but this does not mean that you have all day. An overall time limit has been set. Divide the total time (in minutes) by the number of questions to determine the approximate time you have for each question.

5) Do not linger over difficult questions

If you come across a difficult question, mark it with a paper clip (useful to have along) and come back to it when you have been through the booklet. One caution if you do this – be sure to skip a number on your answer sheet as well. Check often to be sure that you have not lost your place and that you are marking in the row numbered the same as the question you are answering.

6) Read the questions

Be sure you know what the question asks! Many capable people are unsuccessful because they failed to *read* the questions correctly.

7) Answer all questions

Unless you have been instructed that a penalty will be deducted for incorrect answers, it is better to guess than to omit a question.

8) Speed tests

It is often better NOT to guess on speed tests. It has been found that on timed tests people are tempted to spend the last few seconds before time is called in marking answers at random – without even reading them – in the hope of picking up a few extra points. To discourage this practice, the instructions may warn you that your score will be "corrected" for guessing. That is, a penalty will be applied. The incorrect answers will be deducted from the correct ones, or some other penalty formula will be used.

9) Review your answers

If you finish before time is called, go back to the questions you guessed or omitted to give them further thought. Review other answers if you have time.

10) Return your test materials

If you are ready to leave before others have finished or time is called, take ALL your materials to the monitor and leave quietly. Never take any test material with you. The monitor can discover whose papers are not complete, and taking a test booklet may be grounds for disqualification.

VIII. EXAMINATION TECHNIQUES

1) Read the general instructions carefully. These are usually printed on the first page of the exam booklet. As a rule, these instructions refer to the timing of the examination; the fact that you should not start work until the signal and must stop work at a signal, etc. If there are any *special* instructions, such as a choice of questions to be answered, make sure that you note this instruction carefully.

2) When you are ready to start work on the examination, that is as soon as the signal has been given, read the instructions to each question booklet, underline any key words or phrases, such as *least, best, outline, describe* and the like. In this way you will tend to answer as requested rather than discover on reviewing your paper that you *listed without describing*, that you selected the *worst* choice rather than the *best* choice, etc.

3) If the examination is of the objective or multiple-choice type – that is, each question will also give a series of possible answers: A, B, C or D, and you are called upon to select the best answer and write the letter next to that answer on your answer paper – it is advisable to start answering each question in turn. There may be anywhere from 50 to 100 such questions in the three or four hours allotted and you can see how much time would be taken if you read through all the questions before beginning to answer any. Furthermore, if you come across a question or group of questions which you know would be difficult to answer, it would undoubtedly affect your handling of all the other questions.

4) If the examination is of the essay type and contains but a few questions, it is a moot point as to whether you should read all the questions before starting to answer any one. Of course, if you are given a choice – say five out of seven and the like – then it is essential to read all the questions so you can eliminate the two that are most difficult. If, however, you are asked to answer all the questions, there may be danger in trying to answer the easiest one first because you may find that you will spend too much time on it. The best technique is to answer the first question, then proceed to the second, etc.

5) Time your answers. Before the exam begins, write down the time it started, then add the time allowed for the examination and write down the time it must be completed, then divide the time available somewhat as follows:
   - If 3-1/2 hours are allowed, that would be 210 minutes. If you have 80 objective-type questions, that would be an average of 2-1/2 minutes per question. Allow yourself no more than 2 minutes per question, or a total of 160 minutes, which will permit about 50 minutes to review.
   - If for the time allotment of 210 minutes there are 7 essay questions to answer, that would average about 30 minutes a question. Give yourself only 25 minutes per question so that you have about 35 minutes to review.

6) The most important instruction is to *read each question* and make sure you know what is wanted. The second most important instruction is to *time yourself properly* so that you answer every question. The third most

important instruction is to *answer every question.* Guess if you have to but include something for each question. Remember that you will receive no credit for a blank and will probably receive some credit if you write something in answer to an essay question. If you guess a letter – say "B" for a multiple-choice question – you may have guessed right. If you leave a blank as an answer to a multiple-choice question, the examiners may respect your feelings but it will not add a point to your score. Some exams may penalize you for wrong answers, so in such cases *only*, you may not want to guess unless you have some basis for your answer.

7) Suggestions
   a. Objective-type questions
     1. Examine the question booklet for proper sequence of pages and questions
     2. Read all instructions carefully
     3. Skip any question which seems too difficult; return to it after all other questions have been answered
     4. Apportion your time properly; do not spend too much time on any single question or group of questions
     5. Note and underline key words – *all, most, fewest, least, best, worst, same, opposite*, etc.
     6. Pay particular attention to negatives
     7. Note unusual option, e.g., unduly long, short, complex, different or similar in content to the body of the question
     8. Observe the use of "hedging" words – *probably, may, most likely*, etc.
     9. Make sure that your answer is put next to the same number as the question
     10. Do not second-guess unless you have good reason to believe the second answer is definitely more correct
     11. Cross out original answer if you decide another answer is more accurate; do not erase until you are ready to hand your paper in
     12. Answer all questions; guess unless instructed otherwise
     13. Leave time for review

   b. Essay questions
     1. Read each question carefully
     2. Determine exactly what is wanted. Underline key words or phrases.
     3. Decide on outline or paragraph answer
     4. Include many different points and elements unless asked to develop any one or two points or elements
     5. Show impartiality by giving pros and cons unless directed to select one side only
     6. Make and write down any assumptions you find necessary to answer the questions
     7. Watch your English, grammar, punctuation and choice of words
     8. Time your answers, don't crowd material

8) Answering the essay question

Most essay questions can be answered by framing the specific response around several key words or ideas. Here are a few such key words or ideas:

M's: manpower, materials, methods, money, management

P's: purpose, program, policy, plan, procedure, practice, problems, pitfalls, personnel, public relations

    a. Six basic steps in handling problems:
1. Preliminary plan and background development
2. Collect information, data and facts
3. Analyze and interpret information, data and facts
4. Analyze and develop solutions as well as make recommendations
5. Prepare report and sell recommendations
6. Install recommendations and follow up effectiveness

    b. Pitfalls to avoid
1. *Taking things for granted* – A statement of the situation does not necessarily imply that each of the elements is necessarily true; for example, a complaint may be invalid and biased so that all that can be taken for granted is that a complaint has been registered
2. *Considering only one side of a situation* – Wherever possible, indicate several alternatives and then point out the reasons you selected the best one
3. *Failing to indicate follow up* – Whenever your answer indicates action on your part, make certain that you will take proper follow-up action to see how successful your recommendations, procedures or actions turn out to be
4. *Taking too long in answering any single question* – Remember to time your answers properly

IX. AFTER THE TEST

Scoring procedures differ in detail among civil service jurisdictions although the general principles are the same. Whether the papers are hand-scored or graded by machine we have described, they are nearly always graded by number. That is, the person who marks the paper knows only the number – never the name – of the applicant. Not until all the papers have been graded will they be matched with names. If other tests, such as training and experience or oral interview ratings have been given, scores will be combined. Different parts of the examination usually have different weights. For example, the written test might count 60 percent of the final grade, and a rating of training and experience 40 percent. In many jurisdictions, veterans will have a certain number of points added to their grades.

After the final grade has been determined, the names are placed in grade order and an eligible list is established. There are various methods for resolving ties between those who get the same final grade – probably the most common is to place first the name of the person whose application was received first. Job offers are made from the eligible list in the order the names appear on it. You will be notified of your grade and your rank as soon as all these computations have been made. This will bo dono ac rapidly as possible.

People who are found to meet the requirements in the announcement are called "eligibles." Their names are put on a list of eligible candidates. An eligible's chances of getting a job depend on how high he stands on this list and how fast agencies are filling jobs from the list.

When a job is to be filled from a list of eligibles, the agency asks for the names of people on the list of eligibles for that job. When the civil service commission receives this request, it sends to the agency the names of the three people highest on this list. Or, if the job to be filled has specialized requirements, the office sends the agency the names of the top three persons who meet these requirements from the general list.

The appointing officer makes a choice from among the three people whose names were sent to him. If the selected person accepts the appointment, the names of the others are put back on the list to be considered for future openings.

That is the rule in hiring from all kinds of eligible lists, whether they are for typist, carpenter, chemist, or something else. For every vacancy, the appointing officer has his choice of any one of the top three eligibles on the list. This explains why the person whose name is on top of the list sometimes does not get an appointment when some of the persons lower on the list do. If the appointing officer chooses the second or third eligible, the No. 1 eligible does not get a job at once, but stays on the list until he is appointed or the list is terminated.

X. HOW TO PASS THE INTERVIEW TEST

The examination for which you applied requires an oral interview test. You have already taken the written test and you are now being called for the interview test – the final part of the formal examination.

You may think that it is not possible to prepare for an interview test and that there are no procedures to follow during an interview. Our purpose is to point out some things you can do in advance that will help you and some good rules to follow and pitfalls to avoid while you are being interviewed.

What is an interview supposed to test?

The written examination is designed to test the technical knowledge and competence of the candidate; the oral is designed to evaluate intangible qualities, not readily measured otherwise, and to establish a list showing the relative fitness of each candidate – as measured against his competitors – for the position sought. Scoring is not on the basis of "right" and "wrong," but on a sliding scale of values ranging from "not passable" to "outstanding." As a matter of fact, it is possible to achieve a relatively low score without a single "incorrect" answer because of evident weakness in the qualities being measured.

Occasionally, an examination may consist entirely of an oral test – either an individual or a group oral. In such cases, information is sought concerning the technical knowledges and abilities of the candidate, since there has been no written examination for this purpose. More commonly, however, an oral test is used to supplement a written examination.

Who conducts interviews?

The composition of oral boards varies among different jurisdictions. In nearly all, a representative of the personnel department serves as chairman. One of the members of the board may be a representative of the department in which the candidate would work. In some cases, "outside experts" are used, and, frequently, a businessman or some other representative of the general public is asked to serve. Labor and management or other special groups may be represented. The aim is to secure the services of experts in the appropriate field.

However the board is composed, it is a good idea (and not at all improper or unethical) to ascertain in advance of the interview who the members are and what groups they represent. When you are introduced to them, you will have some idea of their backgrounds and interests, and at least you will not stutter and stammer over their names.

What should be done before the interview?

While knowledge about the board members is useful and takes some of the surprise element out of the interview, there is other preparation which is more substantive. It *is* possible to prepare for an oral interview – in several ways:

1) Keep a copy of your application and review it carefully before the interview

This may be the only document before the oral board, and the starting point of the interview. Know what education and experience you have listed there, and the sequence and dates of all of it. Sometimes the board will ask you to review the highlights of your experience for them; you should not have to hem and haw doing it.

2) Study the class specification and the examination announcement

Usually, the oral board has one or both of these to guide them. The qualities, characteristics or knowledges required by the position sought are stated in these documents. They offer valuable clues as to the nature of the oral interview. For example, if the job involves supervisory responsibilities, the announcement will usually indicate that knowledge of modern supervisory methods and the qualifications of the candidate as a supervisor will be tested. If so, you can expect such questions, frequently in the form of a hypothetical situation which you are expected to solve. NEVER go into an oral without knowledge of the duties and responsibilities of the job you seek.

3) Think through each qualification required

Try to visualize the kind of questions you would ask if you were a board member. How well could you answer them? Try especially to appraise your own knowledge and background in each area, *measured against the job sought*, and identify any areas in which you are weak. Be critical and realistic – do not flatter yourself.

4) Do some general reading in areas in which you feel you may be weak

For example, if the job involves supervision and your past experience has NOT, some general reading in supervisory methods and practices, particularly in the field of human relations, might be useful. Do NOT study agency procedures or detailed manuals. The oral board will be testing your understanding and capacity, not your memory.

5) Get a good night's sleep and watch your general health and mental attitude

You will want a clear head at the interview. Take care of a cold or any other minor ailment, and of course, no hangovers.

What should be done on the day of the interview?

Now comes the day of the interview itself. Give yourself plenty of time to get there. Plan to arrive somewhat ahead of the scheduled time, particularly if your appointment is in the fore part of the day. If a previous candidate fails to appear, the board might be ready for you a bit early. By early afternoon an oral board is almost invariably behind schedule if there are many candidates, and you may have to wait.

Take along a book or magazine to read, or your application to review, but leave any extraneous material in the waiting room when you go in for your interview. In any event, relax and compose yourself.

The matter of dress is important. The board is forming impressions about you – from your experience, your manners, your attitude, and your appearance. Give your personal appearance careful attention. Dress your best, but not your flashiest. Choose conservative, appropriate clothing, and be sure it is immaculate. This is a business interview, and your appearance should indicate that you regard it as such. Besides, being well groomed and properly dressed will help boost your confidence.

Sooner or later, someone will call your name and escort you into the interview room. *This is it.* From here on you are on your own. It is too late for any more preparation. But remember, you asked for this opportunity to prove your fitness, and you are here because your request was granted.

What happens when you go in?

The usual sequence of events will be as follows: The clerk (who is often the board stenographer) will introduce you to the chairman of the oral board, who will introduce you to the other members of the board. Acknowledge the introductions before you sit down. Do not be surprised if you find a microphone facing you or a stenotypist sitting by. Oral interviews are usually recorded in the event of an appeal or other review.

Usually the chairman of the board will open the interview by reviewing the highlights of your education and work experience from your application – primarily for the benefit of the other members of the board, as well as to get the material into the record. Do not interrupt or comment unless there is an error or significant misinterpretation; if that is the case, do not hesitate. But do not quibble about insignificant matters. Also, he will usually ask you some question about your education, experience or your present job – partly to get you to start talking and to establish the interviewing "rapport." He may start the actual questioning, or turn it over to one of the other members. Frequently, each member undertakes the questioning on a particular area, one in which he is perhaps most competent, so you can expect each member to participate in the examination. Because time is limited, you may also expect some rather abrupt switches in the direction the questioning takes, so do not be upset by it. Normally, a board member will not pursue a single line of questioning unless he discovers a particular strength or weakness.

After each member has participated, the chairman will usually ask whether any member has any further questions, then will ask you if you have anything you wish to add. Unless you are expecting this question, it may floor you. Worse, it may start you off on an extended, extemporaneous speech. The board is not usually seeking more information. The question is principally to offer you a last opportunity to present further qualifications or to indicate that you have nothing to add. So, if you feel that a significant qualification or characteristic has been overlooked, it is proper to point it out in a sentence or so. Do not compliment the board on the thoroughness of their examination – they have been sketchy, and you know it. If you wish, merely say, "No thank you, I have nothing further to add." This is a point where you can "talk yourself out" of a good impression or fail to present an important bit of information. Remember, *you close the interview yourself.*

The chairman will then say, "That is all, Mr. _____, thank you." Do not be startled; the interview is over, and quicker than you think. Thank him, gather your belongings and take your leave. Save your sigh of relief for the other side of the door.

How to put your best foot forward

Throughout this entire process, you may feel that the board individually and collectively is trying to pierce your defenses, seek out your hidden weaknesses and embarrass and confuse you. Actually, this is not true. They are obliged to make an appraisal of your qualifications for the job you are seeking, and they want to see you in your best light. Remember, they must interview all candidates and a non-cooperative candidate may become a failure in spite of their best efforts to bring out his qualifications. Here are 15 suggestions that will help you:

1) Be natural – Keep your attitude confident, not cocky

If you are not confident that you can do the job, do not expect the board to be. Do not apologize for your weaknesses, try to bring out your strong points. The board is interested in a positive, not negative, presentation. Cockiness will antagonize any board member and make him wonder if you are covering up a weakness by a false show of strength.

2) Get comfortable, but don't lounge or sprawl

Sit erectly but not stiffly. A careless posture may lead the board to conclude that you are careless in other things, or at least that you are not impressed by the importance of the occasion. Either conclusion is natural, even if incorrect. Do not fuss with your clothing, a pencil or an ashtray. Your hands may occasionally be useful to emphasize a point; do not let them become a point of distraction.

3) Do not wisecrack or make small talk

This is a serious situation, and your attitude should show that you consider it as such. Further, the time of the board is limited – they do not want to waste it, and neither should you.

4) Do not exaggerate your experience or abilities

In the first place, from information in the application or other interviews and sources, the board may know more about you than you think. Secondly, you probably will not get away with it. An experienced board is rather adept at spotting such a situation, so do not take the chance.

5) If you know a board member, do not make a point of it, yet do not hide it

Certainly you are not fooling him, and probably not the other members of the board. Do not try to take advantage of your acquaintanceship – it will probably do you little good.

6) Do not dominate the interview

Let the board do that. They will give you the clues – do not assume that you have to do all the talking. Realize that the board has a number of questions to ask you, and do not try to take up all the interview time by showing off your extensive knowledge of the answer to the first one.

7) Be attentive

You only have 20 minutes or so, and you should keep your attention at its sharpest throughout. When a member is addressing a problem or question to you, give him your undivided attention. Address your reply principally to him, but do not exclude the other board members.

8) Do not interrupt

A board member may be stating a problem for you to analyze. He will ask you a question when the time comes. Let him state the problem, and wait for the question.

9) Make sure you understand the question

Do not try to answer until you are sure what the question is. If it is not clear, restate it in your own words or ask the board member to clarify it for you. However, do not haggle about minor elements.

10) Reply promptly but not hastily

A common entry on oral board rating sheets is "candidate responded readily," or "candidate hesitated in replies." Respond as promptly and quickly as you can, but do not jump to a hasty, ill-considered answer.

11) Do not be peremptory in your answers

A brief answer is proper – but do not fire your answer back. That is a losing game from your point of view. The board member can probably ask questions much faster than you can answer them.

12) Do not try to create the answer you think the board member wants

He is interested in what kind of mind you have and how it works – not in playing games. Furthermore, he can usually spot this practice and will actually grade you down on it.

13) Do not switch sides in your reply merely to agree with a board member

Frequently, a member will take a contrary position merely to draw you out and to see if you are willing and able to defend your point of view. Do not start a debate, yet do not surrender a good position. If a position is worth taking, it is worth defending.

14) Do not be afraid to admit an error in judgment if you are shown to be wrong

The board knows that you are forced to reply without any opportunity for careful consideration. Your answer may be demonstrably wrong. If so, admit it and get on with the interview.

15) Do not dwell at length on your present job

The opening question may relate to your present assignment. Answer the question but do not go into an extended discussion. You are being examined for a *new* job, not your present one. As a matter of fact, try to phrase ALL your answers in terms of the job for which you are being examined.

Basis of Rating

Probably you will forget most of these "do's" and "don'ts" when you walk into the oral interview room. Even remembering them all will not ensure you a passing grade. Perhaps you did not have the qualifications in the first place. But remembering them will help you to put your best foot forward, without treading on the toes of the board members.

Rumor and popular opinion to the contrary notwithstanding, an oral board wants you to make the best appearance possible. They know you are under pressure – but they also want to see how you respond to it as a guide to what your reaction would be under the pressures of the job you seek. They will be influenced by the degree of poise you display, the personal traits you show and the manner in which you respond.

EXAMINATION SECTION

EXAMINATION SECTION
TEST 1

DIRECTIONS: Each question or incomplete statement is followed by several suggested answers or completions. Select the one that BEST answers the question or completes the statement. *PRINT THE LETTER OF THE CORRECT ANSWER IN THE SPACE AT THE RIGHT.*

1. Before starting any lawn mowing, the distance between the blade and a flat surface should be measured with a ruler. This distance should be such that the cut of the grass above the ground is _____ inch(es).

    A. 1   B. 1 1/2   C. 2   D. 3

1.____

2. Strainers in a number 6 fuel oil system should be checked once a

    A. day   B. week   C. month   D. year

2.____

3. The spinning cup on a rotary cup oil burner should be cleaned once

    A. a day   B. a week
    C. every two weeks   D. a month

3.____

4. Terrazzo floors should be cleaned daily with a

    A. damp mop using clear water
    B. damp mop using a strong alkaline solution
    C. damp mop using a mild acid solution
    D. dust mop treated with vegetable oil

4.____

5. New installations of vinyl-asbestos floors should

    A. never be machine scrubbed
    B. be dry-buffed weekly
    C. be swept daily, using an oily compound
    D. never be swept with treated dust mops

5.____

6. Standpipe fire hose shall be inspected

    A. monthly   B. quarterly
    C. semi-annually   D. annually

6.____

7. All portable fire extinguishers shall be inspected once

    A. a year   B. a month
    C. a week   D. every 3 months

7.____

8. Soda-acid and foam-type fire extinguishers shall be discharged and recharged at least once

    A. each year   B. every two years
    C. every six months   D. each month

8.____

9. Elevator *safeties* under the car shall be tested once each

    A. day   B. week   C. month   D. quarter

9.____

10. Key-type fire alarms in public school buildings shall be tested   10.___

    A. daily   B. weekly
    C. monthly   D. quarterly

11. Combustion efficiency can be determined from an appropriate chart used in conjunction   11.___
    with _____ temperature and

    A. steam; steam pressure
    B. flue gas; percentage of CO_2
    C. flue gas; fuel heating value
    D. oil; steam pressure

12. In the combustion of common fuels, the major boiler heat loss is due to   12.___

    A. incomplete combustion
    B. moisture in the fuel
    C. heat radiation
    D. heat lost in the flue gases

13. The MOST important reason for blowing down a boiler water column and gauge glass is   13.___
    to

    A. prevent the gauge glass level from rising too high
    B. relieve stresses in the gauge glass
    C. insure a true water level reading
    D. insure a true pressure gauge reading

14. The secondary voltage of a transformer used for ignition in a fuel oil burner has a range   14.___
    of MOST NEARLY _____ volts to _____ volts.

    A. 120; 240   B. 440; 660
    C. 660; 1,200   D. 5,000; 15,000

15. Assume that during the month of April there were 3 days with an average outdoor tem-   15.___
    perature of 30° F, 7 days with 40° F, 10 days with 50° F, 3 days with 60° F, and 7 days with
    65° F.
    The number of degree days for the month was

    A. 330   B. 445   C. 595   D. 1,150

16. The pH of boiler feedwater is usually maintained within the range of   16.___

    A. 4 to 5   B. 6 to 7   C. 10 to 12   D. 13 to 14

17. The admission of steam to the coils of a domestic hot water supply tank is regulated by   17.___
    a(n)

    A. pressure regulating valve
    B, immersion type temperature gauge
    C. check valve
    D. thermostatic control valve

18. The device which senses primary air failure in a rotary cup oil burner is usually called   18.____
a(n)

    A. vaporstat   B. anemometer
    C. venturi   D. pressure gauge

19. The device which starts and stops the flow of oil into an automatic rotary cup oil burner is   19.____
usually called a(n) _____ valve.

    A. magnetic oil   B. oil metering
    C. oil check   D. relief

20. A vacuum breaker, used on a steam heated domestic hot water tank, is usually con-   20.____
nected to the

    A. circulating pump   B. tank wall
    C. aquastat   D. steam coil flange

21. A vacuum pump in a low pressure steam heating system which is equipped with a float   21.____
switch, a vacuum switch, a magnetic starter, and a selector switch can be operated on

    A. float, vacuum, or automatic
    B. float, vacuum, or continuous
    C. vacuum, automatic, or continuous
    D. float, automatic, or continuous

22. If the temperature of the condensate returning to the vacuum pump in a low pressure   22.____
steam vacuum heating system is above 180° F, the trouble may be caused by

    A. faulty radiator traps
    B. room thermostats being set too high
    C. uninsulated return lines
    D. too many radiators being shut off

23. A feedwater regulator operates to   23.____

    A. shut down the burner when the water is low
    B. maintain the water in the boiler at a predetermined level
    C. drain the water from the boiler
    D. regulate the temperature of the feedwater

24. An automatically fired steam boiler is equipped with an automatic low water cut-off.   24.____
The low water cut-off is usually actuated by

    A. steam pressure   B. fuel pressure
    C. float action   D. water temperature

25. Low pressure steam or an electric heater is usually required for heating No. _____ fuel   25.____
oil.

    A. 1   B. 2   C. 4   D. 6

KEY (CORRECT ANSWERS)

1.	C	11.	B
2.	A	12.	D
3.	A	13.	C
4.	A	14.	D
5.	B	15.	B
6.	B	16.	C
7.	B	17.	D
8.	A	18.	A
9.	C	19.	A
10.	A	20.	D

21.	D
22.	A
23.	B
24.	C
25.	D

———

TEST 2

DIRECTIONS: Each question or incomplete statement is followed by several suggested answers or completions. Select the one that BEST answers the question or completes the statement. *PRINT THE LETTER OF THE CORRECT ANSWER IN THE SPACE AT THE RIGHT.*

1. A compound gauge is calibrated to read

   A. pressure only
   C. vacuum and pressure

   B. vacuum only
   D. temperature and humidity

   1._____

2. In a mechanical pressure-atomizing type oil burner, the oil is atomized by using an atomizing tip and

   A. steam pressure
   C. compressed air

   B. pump pressure
   D. a spinning cup

   2._____

3. A good over-the-fire draft in a natural draft furnace should be approximately _____ inches of water _____.

   A. 5.0; positive pressure
   C. 0.05; vacuum

   B. 0.05; positive pressure
   D. 5.0; vacuum

   3._____

4. When it is necessary to add chemicals to a heating boiler, it should be done

   A. immediately after boiler blowdown
   B. after the boiler has been cleaned internally of sludge, scale, and other foreign matter
   C. at periods when condensate flow to the boiler is small
   D. at a time when there is a heavy flow of condensate to the boiler

   4._____

5. The modutrol motor on a rotary cup oil burner burning #6 fuel oil automatically operates the primary air damper,

   A. secondary air damper, and oil metering valve
   B. secondary air damper, and magnetic oil valve
   C. oil metering valve, and magnetic oil valve
   D. and magnetic oil valve

   5._____

6. The manual-reset pressuretrol is classified as a _____ Control.

   A. Safety and Operating
   B. Limit and Operating
   C. Limit and Safety
   D. Limit, Operating, and Safety

   6._____

7. Sodium sulphite is added to boiler feedwater to

   A. avoid caustic embrittlement
   B. increase the pH value
   C. reduce the tendency of foaming in the steam drum
   D. remove dissolved oxygen

   7._____

8. Neat cement is a mixture of cement, 8.___

   A. putty, and water
   C. lime and water
   B. and water
   D. salt, and water

9. In a concrete mix of 1:2:4, the 2 refers to the amount of 9.___

   A. sand
   B. cement
   C. stone
   D. water

10. The word *natatorium* means MOST NEARLY a(n) 10.___

    A. auditorium
    C. gymnasium
    B. playroom
    D. indoor swimming pool

11. Plated metal surfaces which are protected by a thin coat of clear lacquer should be cleaned with a(n) 11.___

    A. abrasive compound
    C. mild soap solution
    B. liquid polish
    D. lemon oil solution

12. Wet mop filler replacements are ordered by 12.___

    A. length
    C. number of strands
    B. weight
    D. trade number

13. The BEST way to determine the value of a cleaning material is by 13.___

    A. performance testing
    B. manufacturer's literature
    C. written specifications
    D. interviews with manufacturer's salesman

14. The instructions on a container of cleaning compound states, *Mix one pound of compound in 5 gallons of water.* Using these instructions, the amount of compound which should be added to 15 quarts of water is MOST likely _____ ounces. 14.___

    A. 3
    B. 8
    C. 12
    D. 48

15. The MOST usual cause of paint blisters is 15.___

    A. too much oil in the paint
    B. moisture under the paint coat
    C. a heavy coat of paint
    D. improper drying of the paint

16. The floor that should NOT be machined scrubbed is a(n) 16.___

    A. lobby
    C. gymnasium
    B. lunchroom
    D. auditorium aisle

17. Pick-up sweeping in a school building is the occasional removal of the more conspicuous loose dirt from corridors and lobbies.
    This type of sweeping should be done 17.___

    A. after scrubbing or waxing of floors
    B. with the aid of a sweeping compound
    C. at night after school hours
    D. during regular school hours

18. According to recommended practice, when a steam boiler is taken out of service for a long period of time, the boiler drums should FIRST be   18.____

    A. drained completely while the water is hot (above 212° F)
    B. drained completely after the water has been cooled down to 180° F
    C. filled completely without draining
    D. filled to the level of the top try cock

19. Specifications concerning window cleaners' anchors and safety belts must be in compliance with the rules and regulations outlined in the   19.____

    A. State Labor Law and Board of Standards and Appeals
    B. Building Code
    C. Fire Department Safety Manual
    D. National Protection Association

20. If it is not possible to plant new shrubs immediately upon delivery in the spring, they should be stored in a(n)   20.____

    A. sheltered outdoor area   B. unsheltered outdoor area
    C. boiler room   D. warm place indoors

21. Peat moss is generally used for its   21.____

    A. food value   B. nitrogen
    C. alkalinity   D. moisture retaining quality

22. The legal minimum age of employees engaged for cleaning windows in the state is _____ years.   22.____

    A. 16   B. 17   C. 18   D. 21

23. Pruning of street trees is the responsibility of the   23.____

    A. School Custodian Engineer
    B. Board of Education
    C. Department of Parks
    D. Borough President's Office

24. The prevention and control of vermin and rodents in a school building is PRIMARILY a matter of   24.____

    A. maintaining good housekeeping on a continuous basis
    B. periodic use of an exterminator's service
    C. calling in the exterminator when necessary
    D. cleaning the building thoroughly during school vacation

25. The MAIN classification of lumber used for construction purposes is known as _____ lumber.   25.____

    A. industrial   B. commercial
    C. finish   D. yard

KEY (CORRECT ANSWERS)

1.	C		11.	C
2.	B		12.	B
3.	C		13.	A
4.	D		14.	C
5.	A		15.	B
6.	C		16.	C
7.	D		17.	D
8.	B		18.	B
9.	A		19.	A
10.	D		20.	A

21.	D
22.	C
23.	C
24.	A
25.	D

TEST 3

DIRECTIONS: Each question or incomplete statement is followed by several suggested answers or completions. Select the one that BEST answers the question or completes the statement. *PRINT THE LETTER OF THE CORRECT ANSWER IN THE SPACE AT THE RIGHT.*

1. Oil-soaked waste and rags should be

    A. deposited in a self-closing metal can
    B. piled in the open
    C. stored in the supply closet
    D. rolled up and be available for the next job

1.____

2. Inspection for safety should be included as part of the custodian engineer's _____ inspection.

    A. daily   B. weekly   C. monthly   D. quarterly

2.____

3. Of the following classifications, the one which pertains to fires in electrical equipment is Class

    A. A   B. B   C. C   D. D

3.____

4. The type of portable fire extinguisher which is PARTICULARLY suited for extinguishing flammable liquid fires is the _____ type.

    A. soda-acid   B. foam
    C. pump tank   D. loaded stream

4.____

5. Of the following liquids, the one which has the LOWEST flash point is

    A. kerosene   B. gasoline
    C. benzene   D. carbon tetrachloride

5.____

6. When giving first aid to an injured person, which one of the following should you NOT do?

    A. Administer medication internally
    B. Send for a physician
    C. Control bleeding
    D. Treat for shock

6.____

7. In reference to firefighting, fires are of such complexity that

    A. no plans or methods of attack can be formulated in advance
    B. the problem must be considered in advance and methods of attack formulated
    C. an appointed committee is necessary to direct fighting at the fire
    D. no planned procedures can be relied on

7.____

8. The heat of a soldering copper should be tested

    A. with colder
    B. by holding it near kraft paper
    C. by holding it near your hand
    D. with water

8.____

9. Safety on the job is BEST assured by   9.___

    A. keeping alert   B. following every rule
    C. working very slowly   D. never working alone

10. One important use of accident reports is to provide information that may be used to   10.___
reduce the possibility of similar accidents.
The MOST valuable entry on the report for this purpose is the

    A. time lost due to accident
    B. date of the occurrence
    C. injury sustained by the victim
    D. cause of the accident

11. If the directions given by your superior are NOT clear, the BEST thing for you to do is to   11.___

    A. ask to have the directions repeated and clarified
    B. proceed to do the work taking a chance on doing the right thing
    C. do nothing until some later time when you can find out exactly what is wanted
    D. ask one of the other men in your crew what he would do under the circumstances

12. Of the following procedures concerning grievances of subordinate personnel, the custo-   12.___
dian engineer should maintain an attitude of

    A. paying little attention to little grievances
    B. being very alert to grievances and make adjustments in existing conditions to
       appease all personnel
    C. knowing the most frequent causes of grievances and strive to prevent them from
       arising
    D. maintaining rigid discipline of a nature that *smooths out* all grievances

13. Of the following, the BEST course of action to take to settle a dispute or conflict between   13.___
two employees is to

    A. insist that the two employees settle the case between themselves
    B. call in each one separately and after hearing their cases presented, decide the
       issue
    C. bring both in for a conference at the same time and make the decision in their pres-
       ence
    D. have both present their points of view and arguments in a written memoranda and
       on this basis make your decision

14. If, as a custodian engineer, you discover an error in your report submitted to the main   14.___
office, you should

    A. do nothing, since it is possible that one error will have little effect on the total report
    B. wait until the error is discovered in the main office and then offer to work overtime
       to correct it
    C. go directly to the supervisor in the main office after working hours and ask him
       unofficially to correct the error
    D. notify the main office immediately so that the error can be corrected, if necessary

15. There are a considerable number of forms and reports to be submitted on schedule by   15.____
the custodian engineer. The advisable method of accomplishing this duty is to

    A. fill out the reports at odd times during the days when you have free time
    B. schedule a definite period of the work week for completing these forms and reports
    C. assign your foreman or cleaner to handle all these forms for you and to have them
       available on time
    D. classify or group the forms and reports and fill out only one of each group and refer
       the other forms or reports to the ones completed

16. A custodian engineer can BEST evaluate the quality of work performed by custodial per-   16.____
sonnel by

    A. periodic inspection of the building's cleanliness
    B. studying the time records of personnel
    C. reviewing the building cleaning expenditures
    D. analyzing complaints of building occupants

17. Assume that you are the custodian engineer and one of your employees wants to talk   17.____
with you about a grievance. Of the following actions, the LEAST desirable action for you
to take is to

    A. listen sympathetically
    B. conduct the discussion openly in the presence of the workforce
    C. try to get his point of view
    D. endeavor to obtain all the facts

18. Of the following factors, the one which is LEAST important in evaluating an employee   18.____
and his work is his

    A. dependability   B. quantity of work done
    C. quality of work done   D. education and training

19. Supervision of a group of people engaged in building cleaning operations should NOT   19.____
include supervision of

    A. time spent in cleaning operations
    B. utilization of official rest and lunch periods
    C. cleaning methods
    D. materials used for various cleaning jobs

20. Of the following methods, the BEST one to utilize in assigning custodial personnel to   20.____
clean a multi-floor school building is to

    A. allow the cleaners to pick their room or area assignments out of a hat
    B. have the supervisor make specific room or area assignments to each cleaner sep-
       arately
    C. rotate room and area assignments daily according to a chart posted on the bulletin
       board
    D. let a different member of the group make the room or area assignments each week

21. Assume that you are the custodian engineer and that you have discovered a bottle of 21.___
    liquor in one of your employee's locker.
    The BEST course of action to take is to

    A. fire him immediately
    B. explain to him that liquor should not be brought into a school building and that a
       repetition may result
    C. in disciplinary action
    D. suspend him until the end of the week and take him back only on a probational
       basis
    E. assemble the staff and tell them they are all equally guilty for not having reported
       the matter to you

22. Of the following items, the one which is the LEAST important in the preparation of a 22.___
    report is that the report

    A. is brief, but to the point
    B. uses the prescribed form if there is one
    C. contains extra copies
    D. is accurate

23. In order to have building employees willing to follow standardized cleaning and mainte- 23.___
    nance procedures, the supervisor must be prepared to

    A. work alongside the employees
    B. demonstrate the reasonableness of the procedures
    C. offer incentive pay for their utilization
    D. allow the employees the free use of the time saved by their adoption

24. Suppose that you are the custodian engineer and one of your employees has gross 24.___
    earnings of $437.10 for the week, all of which is subject to deductions at the rate of 4.8%.
    The amount which should be deducted from the employee's gross earnings for the week
    is MOST NEARLY

    A. $2.10   B. $14.70   C. $17.70   D. $20.97

25. Suppose that you are a custodian engineer and an employee works for you at the rate of 25.___
    $8.70 per hour with time and one-half paid for time worked after 40 hours in one week.
    His gross pay for working 53 hours in one week is MOST NEARLY

    A. $461.10   B. $482.10   C. $487.65   D. $517.65

KEY (CORRECT ANSWERS)

1.	A	11.	A
2.	A	12.	C
3.	C	13.	C
4.	B	14.	D
5.	B	15.	B
6.	A	16.	A
7.	B	17.	B
8.	A	18.	D
9.	A	19.	B
10.	D	20.	B

21.	B
22.	C
23.	B
24.	D
25.	D

TEST 4

DIRECTIONS: Each question or incomplete statement is followed by several suggested answers or completions. Select the one that BEST answers the question or completes the statement. *PRINT THE LETTER OF THE CORRECT ANSWER IN THE SPACE AT THE RIGHT.*

1. The minimum number of gate valves usually required in a by-pass around a steam trap is   1.___

   A.   1   B.   2   C.   3   D.   4

2. A 2-inch standard steel pipe, as compared with a 2-inch extra heavy steel pipe, has the same   2.___

   A.   wall thickness   B.   inside diameter
   C.   outside diameter   D.   weight per linear foot

3. A short piece of pipe with a standard male pipe thread on one end and a locknut thread on the other end is usually called a   3.___

   A.   close nipple   B.   tank nipple
   C.   coupling   D.   union

4. Dies are used by plumbers to   4.___

   A.   ream out the inside of pipes
   B.   thread pipes
   C.   bevel the ends of pipes
   D.   make up solder joints

5. Of the following types of pipe, the one which is MOST brittle is   5.___

   A.   brass   B.   copper
   C.   cast iron   D.   wrought iron

6. The PRIMARY function of a trap in a drainage system is   6.___

   A.   prevent gases from flowing into the building
   B.   produce an efficient flushing action
   C.   prevent articles accidentally dropped into the drainage system from entering the water
   D.   prevent the water backing up

7. If a plumbing fixture is allowed to stand unused for a long time, its trap is opt to lose its seal by   7.___

   A.   evaporation   B.   capillary action
   C.   siphonage   D.   condensation

8. The pipe fitting used to connect a 1 1/4" pipe directly to a 1" pipe in a straight line is called a   8.___

   A.   union   B.   nipple   C.   elbow   D.   reducer

9. The BEST procedure to follow when replacing a blown fuse is to

    A. immediately replace it with the same size fuse
    B. immediately replace it with a larger size fuse
    C. immediately replace it with a smaller size fuse
    D. correct the cause of the fuse failure and replace it with the correct size

9.____

10. The amperage rating of the fuse to be used in an electrical circuit is determined by the

    A. size of the connected load
    B. size of the wire in the circuit
    C. voltage of the circuit
    D. ambient temperature

10.____

11. In a 208-volt, 3-phase, 4-wire circuit, the voltage, in volts, from any line to the grounded neutral is approximately

    A. 208   B. 150   C. 120   D. zero

11.____

12. The device commonly used to change an A.C. voltage to a D.C. voltage is called a

    A. transformer   B. rectifier
    C. relay   D. capacitor or condenser

12.____

13. Where conduit enters a knock-out in an outlet box, it should be provided with a

    A. bushing on the inside and locknut on the outside
    B. locknut on the inside and bushing on the outside
    C. union on the outside and a nipple on the inside
    D. nipple on the outside and a union on the inside

13.____

14. The electric circuit to a ten kilowatt electric hot water heater which is automatically controlled by an aquastat will also require a

    A. transistor   B. choke coil
    C. magnetic contactor   D. limit switch

14.____

15. An electric power consumption meter usually indicates the power used in

    A. watts   B. volt-hours
    C. amperes   D. kilowatt-hours

15.____

16. Of the following sizes of copper wire, the one which can SAFELY carry the GREATEST amount of amperes is

    A. 14 ga. stranded   B. 12 ga. stranded
    C. 12 ga. solid   D. 10 ga. solid

16.____

17. A flexible coupling is PRIMARILY used to

    A. allow for imperfect alignment of two joining shafts
    B. allow for slight differences in shaft diameters
    C. insure perfect alignment of the joining shafts
    D. reduce fast starting of the machinery

17.____

18. The one of the following statements concerning lubricating oil which is CORRECT is: 18.___
    A. SAE 10 is heavier and more viscous than SAE 30
    B. diluting lubricating oil with gasoline increases its viscosity
    C. oil reduces friction between moving parts
    D. in hot weather, thin oil is preferable to heavy oil

19. The MAIN purpose of periodic inspections and tests made on mechanical equipment is   19.___
    to
    A. make the operating men familiar with the equipment
    B. keep the maintenance men busy during otherwise slack periods
    C. discover minor faults before they develop into serious breakdowns
    D. encourage the men to take better care of the equipment

20. The one of the following bearing types which is NOT classified as a roller bearing is   20.___
    A. radial   B. angular   C. thrust   D. babbit

21. In a wire rope, when a number of wires are laid left-handed into a strand and the strand   21.___
    laid right-handed around a hemp rope center, the wire rope is commonly known as a
    _____ rope.
    A. right-lay, Lang-lay   B. left-lay, Lang-lay
    C. left-lay, regular-lay   D. right-lay, regular-lay

22. The chemical which is NOT used for disinfecting swimming pools is   22.___
    A. ammonia   B. calcium hypochlorite
    C. chlorine   D. liquified chlorine

23. The one of the following V-belt sections which has the HIGHEST horsepower-per-belt   23.___
    rating is _____ section.
    A. A   B. B   C. C   D. D

24. An air compressor which is driven by an electric motor is usually started and stopped   24.___
    automatically by a(n)
    A. unloader   B. pressure regulator valve
    C. float switch   D. pressure switch

25. The volume, in cubic feet, of a cylindrical tank, 6 ft. in diameter x 35 ft. long is MOST   25.___
    NEARLY
    A. 210   B. 990   C. 1,260   D. 3,960

KEY (CORRECT ANSWERS)

1.	C	11.	C
2.	C	12.	B
3.	B	13.	A
4.	B	14.	C
5.	C	15.	D
6.	A	16.	D
7.	A	17.	A
8.	D	18.	C
9.	D	19.	C
10.	B	20.	D

21.	D
22.	A
23.	D
24.	D
25.	B

EXAMINATION SECTION
TEST 1

DIRECTIONS: Each question or incomplete statement is followed by several suggested answers or completions. Select the one that BEST answers the question or completes the statement. *PRINT THE LETTER OF THE CORRECT ANSWER IN THE SPACE AT THE RIGHT.*

1. Two cleaners swept four corridors in 24 minutes. Each corridor measured 12 feet x 176   1._____
feet.
The space swept per man per minute was MOST NEARLY _____ square feet.

   A. 50   B. 90   C. 180   D. 350

2. The BEST time of the day to dust classroom furniture and woodwork is   2._____

   A. in the morning before the students arrive
   B. during the morning recess
   C. during the students' lunch time
   D. immediately after the students are dismissed for the day

3. A custodian-engineer wishes to order sponges in the most economical manner.   3._____
Keeping in mind that large sponges can be cut up into many smaller sizes, the one of
the following that has the LEAST cost per cubic inch of sponge is

   A. 2" x 4" x 6" sponges @ $0.24
   B. 4" x 8" x 12" sponges @ $1.44
   C. 4" x 6" x 36" sponges @ $4.80
   D. 6" x 8" x 32" sponges @ $9.60

4. Many new products are used in new schools for floors, walls, and other surfaces.   4._____
A custodian-engineer should determine the BEST procedure to be used to clean such
new surfaces by

   A. referring to the board of education's manual of procedures
   B. obtaining information on the cleaning procedure from the manufacturer
   C. asking the advice of the mechanics who installed the new material
   D. asking the district supervisor how to clean the surfaces

5. The one of the following chemicals that a custodian-engineer should tell a cleaner to use   5._____
to remove mildew from terrazzo is

   A. ammonia   B. oxalic acid
   C. sodium hypochlorite   D. sodium silicate

6. The type of soft floor that is basically a mixture of oxidized linseed oil, resin, and ground   6._____
cork pressed upon a burlap backing is known as

   A. asphalt tile   B. cork tile
   C. linoleum   D. vinyl tile

7. The difficulty of cleaning soil from surfaces is LEAST affected by the   7._____

   A. length of time between cleanings
   B. chemical nature of the soil

C. smoothness of the surface being cleaned
D. standard time allotted to the job

8. The one of the following cleaning agents that is GENERALLY classified as an alkaline cleaner is   8.___

A. sodium carbonate
C. kerosene
B. ground silica
D. lemon oil

9. The one of the following cleaning agents that should be used ONLY when adequate ventilation and protective measures have been taken is   9.___

A. methylene chloride
C. sodium carbonate
B. sodium chloride
D. calcium carbonate

10. Of the following, the MOST important consideration in the selection of a cleaning agent is the   10.___

A. cost per pound or gallon
B. amount of labor involved in its use
C. wording of the manufacturer's warranty
D. length of time the manufacturer has been producing cleaning agents

11. The fan motor in a central vacuum cleaner system is found to be operating at 110% of its rated capacity.   11.___
The one of the following actions which is MOST likely to decrease the load on the motor is

A. tying-back several outlets in the open position on each floor
B. moving the butterfly damper slightly toward the closed position
C. removing ten percent of the filter bags
D. operating the bag shaker continuously

12. A groundskeeper asks how to remove an accumulation of grease from the concrete near the loading dock.   12.___
Of the following, the cleaning agent that a custodian-engineer should tell him to use to degrease the area is a(n)

A. acid cleaner
C. liquid soap
B. alkaline cleaner
D. solvent cleaner

13. The instructions for mixing a powdered cleaner in water state, *Mix three ounces of powder in a 14-quart pail three-quarters full of water.*   13.___
A cleaner asks you how much powdered cleaner he should use in a mop truck containing 28 gallons of water to obtain the same strength solution. Your answer should be _____ ounces of powder.

A. 6   B. 8   C. 24   D. 32

14. A resin-base floor finish USUALLY   14.___

A. gives the highest lustre of all floor finishes
B. should be applied in one heavy coat
C. provides a slip-resistant surface
D. should not be used on asphalt tile

15. The one of the following cleaning operations on soft floors that generally requires MOST NEARLY the same amount of time per 1,000 square feet as damp mopping is
    15.____

    A.   applying a thin coat of wax
    B.   sweeping
    C.   dust mopping
    D.   wet mopping

16. Of the following cleaning jobs, the one that should be allowed the MOST time to complete a 1,000 square foot area is
    16.____

    A.   vacuuming carpets
    B.   washing painted walls
    C.   stripping and waxing soft floors
    D.   machine-scrubbing hard floors

17. When instructing your staff in the use of sodium silicate, you should tell them that it is MOST commonly used to
    17.____

    A.   seal concrete floors
              B.   condition leather
    C.   treat boiler water
                D.   neutralize acid wastes

18. Cleaners should be instructed that dust mopping is LEAST appropriate for removing light soil from _____ floors.
    18.____

    A.   terrazzo
                  B.   unsealed concrete
    C.   resin-finished soft
          D.   sealed wood

19. Of the following, the substance that should be recommended for polishing hardwood furniture is
    19.____

    A.   lemon oil polish
                B.   neat's-foot oil
    C.   paste wax
                D.   water-emulsion wax

20. The use of concentrated acid to remove stains from ceramic tile bathroom floors USUALLY results in making the surface
    20.____

    A.   pitted and porous
           B.   clean and shiny
    C.   harder and glossier
        D.   waterproof

21. Asphalt tile floors should be protected by coating them with
    21.____

    A.   hard-milled soap
          B.   water-emulsion wax
    C.   sodium metaphosphate
      D.   varnish

22. Of the following, the BEST way to economize on cleaning tools and materials is to
    22.____

    A.   train the cleaners to use them properly
    B.   order at least a three-year supply of every item in order to avpid annual price increases
    C.   attach a price sticker to every item so that the people using them will realize their high cost
    D.   delay ordering material for three months at the beginning of each year to be sure that the old material is used to the fullest extent

23. The MINIMUM amount of free chlorine that swimming pool water should contain for proper disinfection is _____ parts per million.

    A. 1.0   B. 10   C. 50   D. 500

23.___

24. The point at which swimming pool filters should be back-washed is when the difference between the inlet and outlet pressures EXCEEDS _____ psi.

    A. 5   B. 10   C. 15   D. 20

24.___

25. An orthotolidine test is used to test a water sample to see what quantity it contains of

    A. alum   B. ammonia   C. chlorine   D. soda ash

25.___

26. The ideal flue gas temperature in a rotary-cup oil-fired boiler should be equal to the steam temperature PLUS

    A. 50° F   B. 125° F   C. 275° F   D. 550° F

26.___

27. The carbon dioxide reading in a boiler flue when the boiler is operating efficiently should be MOST NEARLY

    A. 0.5 inches of water   B. 8 ounces per mol
    C. 10 psi   D. 12 percent

27.___

28. The one of the following that PRIMARILY indicates a low water level in a steam boiler is the

    A. pressure gauge   B. gauge glass
    C. safety valve   D. hydrometer

28.___

29. The one of the following steps that should be taken FIRST if a safety valve on a coal-fired steam boiler pops off is to

    A. add water to the boiler
    B. reduce the draft
    C. tap the side of the safety valve with a mallet
    D. open the bottom blow-off valve

29.___

30. A device that operates to vary the resistance of an electrical circuit is USUALLY part of a _____ pressurtrol.

    A. high-limit   B. low-limit
    C. manual-reset   D. modulating

30.___

KEY (CORRECT ANSWERS)

1.	C	16.	C
2.	A	17.	A
3.	B	18.	B
4.	B	19.	C
5.	C	20.	A
6.	C	21.	B
7.	D	22.	A
8.	A	23.	A
9.	A	24.	B
10.	B	25.	C
11.	B	26.	B
12.	D	27.	D
13.	D	28.	B
14.	C	29.	B
15.	A	30.	D

———

TEST 2

DIRECTIONS: Each question or incomplete statement is followed by several suggested answers or completions. Select the one that BEST answers the question or completes the statement. *PRINT THE LETTER OF THE CORRECT ANSWER IN THE SPACE AT THE RIGHT.*

1. A solenoid valve is actuated by   1._

    A. air pressure   B. electric current
    C. temperature change   D. light rays

2. A sequential draft control on a rotary-cup oil-fired boiler should operate to   2._

    A. *open* the automatic damper at the end of the post-purge perio'd
    B. *open* the automatic damper when the draft has increased during normal burner operation
    C. *close* the automatic damper just before the burner motor starts up
    D. *close* the automatic damper after the burner goes off and the burner cycle is completed

3. The one of the following components of flue gas that indicates, when present, that more   3._
excess air is being supplied than is being used is

    A. carbon dioxide   B. carbon monoxide
    C. nitrogen   D. oxygen

4. An advantage that a float-thermostatic steam trap has over a float-type steam trap of   4._
comparable rating is that a float-thermostatic trap

    A. requires less maintenance
    B. is easier to install
    C. allows non-condensable gases to escape
    D. releases the condensate at a higher temperature

5. A pump delivers 165 pounds of water per minute against a total head of 100 feet.   5._
The water horsepower of this pump is _____ HP.

    A. 1/2   B. 2   C. 5   D. 20

6. Of the following, the BEST instrument to use to measure over-the-fire draft is the   6._

    A. Bourdon tube gauge   B. inclined manometer
    C. mercury manometer   D. potentiometer

7. The temperature of the water in a steam-heated domestic hot water tank is controlled by   7._
a(n)

    A. aquastat   B. thermostatic regulating valve
    C. vacuum breaker   D. thermostatic trap

8. The one of the following conditions that will MOST likely cause fuel oil pressure to fluctu-   8._
ate is

    A. a faulty pressure gauge
    B. a clean oil-strainer
    C. cold oil in the suction line
    D. an over-tight pump drive belt

9. The cooler in a Freon 12 refrigeration system that is equipped with automatic protective   9.____
   devices is MOST likely to be accidentally damaged by water freeze-up when the sys-
   tem('s)

   A. is operating at reduced load
   B. is operating at rated load
   C. condenser water-flow is interrupted
   D. is being pumped down

10. The capacity of a water-cooled condenser is LEAST affected by the   10.____

    A. water temperature
    B. refrigerant temperature
    C. surrounding air temperature
    D. quantity of condenser water being circulated

11. Of the following chemicals used in boiler feedwater treatment, the one that should be   11.____
    used to RETARD corrosion in the boiler circuit due to dissolved oxygen is sodium

    A. aluminate   B. carbonate   C. phosphate   D. sulfite

12. The heating system in a certain school is equipped with vacuum return condensate   12.____
    pumps.
    The MOST likely place for an air-vent valve to be installed in this plant is on

    A. each radiator
    B. the outlet of the domestic hot water steam heating coil
    C. the pressure side of the vacuum pump
    D. the shell of the domestic hot water tank

13. *Priming* of a steam boiler is NOT caused by   13.____

    A. load swings
    B. uneven fire distribution
    C. too high a water level
    D. high alkalinity of the boiler water

14. A Hartford loop is used in school heating systems PRIMARILY to   14.____

    A. provide for thermal expansion of the steam distribution piping
    B. equalize the water level in two or more boilers
    C. prevent siphoning of water out of the boiler
    D. by-pass the electric fuel-oil heaters when the steam heaters are operating

15. Of the following, the MOST likely use for temperature-indicating crayons by a custodian-   15.____
    engineer is in

    A. checking the operation of the radiator traps
    B. replacing room thermometers that have been vandalized
    C. indicating possible sources of spontaneous combustion
    D. checking the effectiveness of an insulating panel

16. A stop-and-waste cock is GENERALLY used on 16.___

    A. refrigerant lines between the compressor and the condenser
    B. soil lines
    C. gas supply lines
    D. water lines subjected to low temperatures

17. A pressure-regulating valve in a compressed air line should be preceded by a(n) 17.___

    A. check valve   B. intercooler
    C. needle valve   D. water-and-oil separator

18. A house trap is a fitting placed in the house drain immediately inside the foundation wall 18.___
of a building.
The MAIN purpose of a house trap is to

    A. prevent the entrance of sewer gas into the building drainage system
    B. provide access to the drain lines in the basement for cleaning
    C. drain the basement in case of flooding
    D. maintain balanced air pressure in the fixture traps

19. The one of the following that is BEST to use to smooth a commutator is 19.___

    A. Number 1/0 emery cloth   B. Number 00 sandpaper
    C. Number 2 steel wool   D. a safe edge file

20. The electric service that is provided to MOST schools in the city is NOMINALLY 20.___

    A. 208 volt-3 phase -4 wire - 120 volts to ground
    B. 208 volt-3 phase -3 wire - 208 volts to ground
    C. 220 volt-2 phase -3 wire - 110 volts to ground
    D. 440 volt-3 phase -4 wire - 240 volts to ground

21. All the fuses in an electrical panel are good but the clips on the fuse in circuit No. 1 are 21.___
much hotter than the clips of the other fuses.
Of the following, the MOST likely cause of this condition is that

    A. circuit No. 1 is greatly overloaded
    B. circuit No. 1 is carrying much less than rated load
    C. the room temperature is abnormally high
    D. the fuse in circuit No. 1 is very loose in its clips

22. Of the following, the BEST tool to use to drive a lag screw is a(n) 22.___

    A. open-end wrench   B. Stillson wrench
    C. screwdriver   D. alien wrench

23. Of the following, the one that is MOST likely to be used in landscaping work as ground 23.___
cover is

    A. Barberry   B. Forsythia
    C. Pachysandra   D. Viburnum

24. The velocity of air in a ventilation duct is USUALLY measured with a(n) 24.___

    A. hydrometer   B. psychrometer
    C. pyrometer   D. pitot tube

25. The motor driving a centrifugal pump through a direct-connected flexible coupling burned out.
When a new motor is ordered, it is important to specify the same NEMA frame size so that the

    A. horsepower will be the same
    B. speed will be the same
    C. conduit box will be in the same location
    D. mounting dimensions will be the same

25.____

26. A custodian-engineer should inspect the school building for safety

    A. at least once each day
    B. at least every other day
    C. at least once a week
    D. at the end of each vacation period

26.____

27. Of the following, the MOST important practice to follow in order to prevent fires in a school is to train the staff to

    A. fight fires of every kind
    B. detect and eliminate every possible fire hazard
    C. keep halls, corridors, and exits clear
    D. place flammables in fire-proof containers

27.____

28. The one of the following types of portable fire extinguishers that is MOST effective in fighting an oil fire is the _____ type.

    A. soda-acid   B. loaded-stream
    C. foam   D. carbon dioxide

28.____

29. A custodian-engineer opens the door to the boiler room and discovers that fuel oil has leaked onto the floor and caught fire.
Of the following, the FIRST action he should take is to

    A. notify the Principal
    B. notify the fire department
    C. turn off the remote control switch
    D. fight the fire using a Class B extinguisher

29.____

30. The MINIMUM noise level beyond which hearing may be impaired is _____ decibels.

    A. 10   B. 50   C. 90   D. 130

30.____

KEY (CORRECT ANSWERS)

1.	B		16.	D
2.	D		17.	D
3.	D		18.	A
4.	C		19.	B
5.	A		20.	A
6.	B		21.	D
7.	B		22.	A
8.	C		23.	C
9.	D		24.	D
10.	C		25.	D
11.	D		26.	A
12.	B		27.	B
13.	D		28.	C
14.	C		29.	C
15.	A		30.	C

———

EXAMINATION SECTION
TEST 1

DIRECTIONS: Each question or incomplete statement is followed by several suggested answers or completions. Select the one that BEST answers the question or completes the statement. *PRINT THE LETTER OF THE CORRECT ANSWER IN THE SPACE AT THE RIGHT.*

1. A boiler horse power is defined as the evaporation of _____ pounds of water per hour, from and at, 212° F.

   A. 32.0   B. 14.7   C. 34.5   D. 29.9

1.____

2. The steam drum of a water tube boiler is 16 feet long and 42" in diameter. Assuming that the normal water line is at the drum centerline, the water content of the drum under normal operating conditions is *most nearly*

   A. 700 gallons
   B. 600 gallons
   C. 400 gallons
   D. 400 cubic feet

2.____

3. In selecting a coal from its "Proximate Analysis," which of the following coals would you consider to be best suited for use in a boiler plant in a heavily populated city?

   A. 7% ash - 18% volatile matter
   B. 10% ash - 21% volatile matter
   C. 12% ash - 17% volatile matter
   D. 5% ash - 25% volatile matter

3.____

4. Which of the following types of grates should be used for ease in cleaning fires, when hand-firing large boilers with #1 buckwheat, under natural draft at heavy loads?

   A. Dumping grates
   B. Stationary grates with 3/4" air spaces
   C. Stationary grates (pin hole type)
   D. Shaking grates

4.____

5. Which of the following fuels contains the *greatest* number of heat units per pound?

   A. Hard coal
   B. No. 6 Fuel Oil
   C. Yard screenings
   D. Bituminous coal

5.____

6. In the usual water tube boiler plant using coal under natural draft, the point where the *maximum* negative draft gauge reading may be obtained is

   A. at the top of the stack
   B. at the base of the stack
   C. over the fire
   D. in the last pass

6.____

7. The purpose of admitting air over the fire in a coal-fired furnace is *usually* to   7.___

    A. reduce the stack gas temperature
    B. improve the draft
    C. reduce the smoke
    D. reduce the draft

8. With steam at a temperature of 365° F in a boiler, which of the following stack gas temperatures would you consider to be *good* usual operating practice in a plant without economizers, air preheaters and the like?   8.___

    A. 300° F   B. 500° F   C. 700° F   D. 900° F

9. The percentage of CO_2 in the stack gases is an indication of the   9.___

    A. rate of combustion in the furnace
    B. rate at which excess air is supplied to the furnace
    C. rate of carbon monoxide production in the furnace
    D. temperature of combustion

10. In the most usual type of large capacity oil burner using #6 oil, under "fully automatic" control, the atomization of the oil is produced MAINLY by the   10.___

    A. pressure from the pump
    B. pressure from the secondary air fan
    C. oil temperature from the heater
    D. rotation of the burner assembly by the motor

11. Of the following, the figure which comes the *closest* to indicating the number of degree days in a normal heating season in New York City is   11.___

    A. 3000   B. 4000   C. 5000   D. 6000

12. In which of the following steam generation methods would you expect to obtain reasonably continuous values of CO_2 *closest* to the perfect CO_2 value?   12.___

    A. Automatic stoker firing with temperature recorder
    B. Automatic stoker firing with "Hold fire timer"
    C. Automatic oil firing with "Stack switch"
    D. Automatic oil firing with "haze regulator"

13. The loss of heat in stack gases for heavy fuel oil is HIGHEST when the   13.___

    A. CO_2 content is 12% and the stack temperature is 500°
    B. CO_2 content is 8% and the stack temperature is 600°
    C. CO_2 content is 6% and the stack temperature is 700°
    D. CO_2 content is 14% and the stack temperature is 600°

14. A badly sooted HRT boiler under coal firing will show   14.___

    A. a higher CO_2 value than a clean boiler
    B. a lower CO_2 value than a clean boiler

C. a higher stack temperature than a clean boiler
D. a lower draft loss than a clean boiler

15. A unit heater condensing 50 lbs. of low pressure steam per hour would be rated *most nearly* at _____ square feet E.D.R.

    A. 50   B. 100   C. 150   D. 200

15.____

16. One horsepower most nearly equals

    A. 550 ft - lbs per sec.
    B. 3300 ft - lbs per min.
    C. 55000 ft - lbs per hour
    D. 10000 ft-lbs per min.

16.____

17. An indicator card from a steam engine is MOST useful to the custodian-engineer in

    A. determining the boiler pressure
    B. determining the engine speed
    C. adjusting the valve setting
    D. computing the mechanical efficiency

17.____

18. Which one of the following statements is *most nearly* correct?

    A. A water tube boiler has the combustion gases inside the tubes
    B. A scotch marine boiler has two drums
    C. A brick set HRT boiler usually has a steel fire box
    D. The circulation in a boiler may be either gravity or forced

18.____

19. When the load on a mechanical stoker fired boiler plant furnishing steam for slide valve engine generators drops by 30%, the

    A. stoker should be shut down
    B. fan should be speeded up and the stoker slowed
    C. stoker should be speeded up and the air supply reduced
    D. stoker speed and air supply should be adjusted by reducing both

19.____

20. Which of the following statements is *most nearly* correct?

    A. All types of mechanical stokers may be used with equal efficiency under all types of boilers
    B. Most stokers are designed with a weak member
    C. The best type of stoker to use is not dependent upon the type of fuel available
    D. Advisability of installing stokers is not dependent upon the load

20.____

21. The number and size of safety valves required on a high pressure boiler is dependent upon the

    A. size of the boiler drums
    B. amount of heating surface
    C. number of pounds of fuel burned per square foot of grate per hour
    D. size of the steam main

21.____

22. In changing over a boiler from high pressure (150 lbs. per square inch) to 10 pounds per square inch, it is usually necessary to

    A. increase the size of the safety valves
    B. decrease the grate area
    C. increase the size of the feed water piping
    D. increase the size of the blow down piping

23. A boiler feed injector becomes temporarily steam bound. To correct this condition, the MOST proper action to take is to

    A. increase boiler pressure
    B. reduce suction lift
    C. wrap it with cold rags
    D. bank fire

24. If the volume of air in cubic feet per minute for combustion is represented by X, which of the following values of X would *most nearly* represent the Cfm of stack gas, under usual conditions, that an induced draft fan would have to handle?

    A. X   B. 2X   C. 3X   D. 4X

25. If the stock switch of an oil burner becomes excessively sooted, a condition *most likely* to result is

    A. continuous shutting down of the burner shortly after it starts up
    B. excessive flow of oil to the burner resulting in a smoky fire
    C. excessive fire due to failure to cut off current to the burner motor
    D. failure of the warp switch of the relay to operate

KEY (CORRECT ANSWERS)

1. C		11. C	
2. B		12. D	
3. A		13. C	
4. A		14. C	
5. B		15. D	
6. B		16. A	
7. C		17. C	
8. B		18. D	
9. B		19. D	
10. D		20. B	

21. B
22. A
23. C
24. B
25. A

TEST 2

DIRECTIONS: Each question or incomplete statement is followed by several suggested answers or completions. Select the one that BEST answers the question or completes the statement. *PRINT THE LETTER OF THE CORRECT ANSWER IN THE SPACE AT THE RIGHT.*

1. In high pressure electric generating plants in large buildings, heating the feed water from 70° F to 180° F with exhaust steam usually will *decrease* the fuel consumption by   1._____

    A. 5%   B. 10%   C. 15%   D. 20%

2. The direct room radiator with a pneumatically controlled steam heating system is cold, while the adjoining rooms are heated adequately.   2._____
Of the following, the FIRST thing you would check in the room is the

    A. steam pipe in the room before the pneumatic steam valve
    B. thermostat
    C. pneumatic steam valve
    D. thermostatic trap

3. The usual vacuum gage on a steam heating system reads in   3._____

    A. inches of vacuum
    B. feet of mercury
    C. inches of water
    D. feet of water

4. In a mechanical pressure type burner using #6 oil heated to 230°F by steam, the oil is atomized by   4._____

    A. centrifugal force
    B. steam temperature
    C. oil temperature
    D. oil pressure

5. A vaporstat with separate motor driven oil pump used on a fully automatic heavy oil burning rotary cup installation is *generally* used to   5._____

    A. keep the boiler pressure within proper limits
    B. regulate the pressure of the primary air
    C. regulate the pressure of the secondary air
    D. shut down the burner when primary air failure occurs

6. In estimating the amount of work being done by a steam driven water pump, the one of the following items which is usually the MOST important in the calculation of pump horsepower is the   6._____

    A. temperature of the water
    B. suction lift
    C. steam pressure
    D. gallons pumped

7. The term "fixture unit" *usually* refers to   7.___

    A. the number of lamp sockets in an electric lighting fixture
    B. the number of fixtures in a room or building
    C. a rate of flow
    D. amperes per second

8. When pumping water from a return tank, equipped with an automatic make up valve   8.___
    located below the pump, the *most probable* cause of periodic pump failures to deliver the
    water, would be

    A. a leak in the suction line
    B. the water was too hot
    C. there was too much water in the tank
    D. a leak in the discharge line

9. Suppose a small oil fire has broken out in the boiler room in your building. Under these   9.___
    circumstances, the extinguisher LEAST suitable for use is

    A. soda-acid   B. pyrene
    C. foamite   D. carbon dioxide

10. Of the following, a low "power factor" would MOST likely result from: 10.___

    A. Corlis valve engine operating at less than 1/2 normal rated load
    B. A large d.c. motor operating at 20% below normal speed
    C. A large induction motor operating at 60% normal rated capacity
    D. A storage battery on which the voltage has dropped to 10% below normal

11. Before putting two d.c. engine generators on the line in parallel, it is usually necessary to   11.___

    A. adjust the speeds so that both are running at exactly the same speed
    B. adjust the loads so that each machine will take its proportionate share
    C. adjust the field of the incoming unit
    D. lower the line voltage

12. Of the following, the BEST type of AC motor to use for direct connection to a timing   12.___
    device which must be very accurate is a

    A. synchronous motor
    B. squirrel cage motor
    C. wound rotor motor
    D. single phase capacitor motor

13. In running temporary electric wiring for a display requiring the use of 30 incandescent 50-   13.___
    watt lamps at the usual lighting voltage, the two main 120V loads supplying this load
    would carry *most nearly* _____ amps.

    A. 23.9   B. 12.5   C. 17.8   D. 9.5

14. One ton of refrigeration may be expressed MOST accurately as   14.___

    A. one ton of ice melting per hour   B. 200 Btu per minute
    C. one horsepower-hour   D. 970 Btu per pound

15. Which of the following statements is correct with respect to filtration plants of swimming   15.____
pools:

    A.   In pressure filter installations a clear well tank is always required as a reservoir of filtered water
    B.   Raw water should be used to backwash filters whenever possible
    C.   The rate of backwashing usually is less than the rate of filtration
    D.   Alum is added to water to form a flee before the water reaches the filters

16. In the operation of a swimming pool, the statement NOT true is: 16.____

    A.   All water supplied must be sterilized at the plant by chemical means
    B.   The pool must be cleaned every third time that it is drained
    C.   The rate of recirculation is dependent upon the size of the pool
    D.   The number of persons permitted to use the pool at any one time determines the rate of recirculation

17. Of the following, the use for which central vacuum cleaning is considered LEAST effec-   17.____
tive is for

    A.   cleaning walls and ceilings
    B.   dusting classroom furniture
    C.   cleaning boiler rooms
    D.   cleaning erasers

18. An electric elevator car stalls on the ground floor of a school building. Of the following,   18.____
the item you would be LEAST likely to check in your inspection is the

    A.   "baby" switch
    B.   floor door switch
    C.   limit switch
    D.   current to elevator motors

19. An examination of the water supply of the sinks of demonstration tables in science rooms   19.____
reveals the use of rubber hose attachments to sink taps extending below the sink rim.
Of the following, the MOST important criticism of this practice is that

    A.   there is greater possibility of water waste through leakage
    B.   the taps may become contaminated by contact with unclean rubber hoses
    C.   a submerged inlet condition may be created resulting in back-siphonage
    D.   a water hammer condition will be created by this elimination of the normal air gap

20. In an investigation of a complaint of sewer gas from a urinal in a regularly used toilet   20.____
room, you find that the trap seal has been lost. The LEAST common cause of this condition is

    A.   evaporation of water from the trap
    B.   vents blocked up
    C.   high wind over roof vent
    D.   self-siphonage

21. A *check* valve in the discharge of a centrifugal pump   21.___

    A. prevents backflow to suction side
    B. keeps the pump primed at all times
    C. eliminates the need for a foot valve
    D. eliminates the need for a gate valve on the pump discharge

22. The modern multiple-circuit program instrument which automatically controls bell signals   22.___
in a school *usually* includes

    A. automatic resetting of electric clocks throughout the school
    B. automatic ringing of room bells when the fire bell switch is closed
    C. prevention of manual control of schedules by eliminating manual control switches
    D. provision for automatic cutout of the schedule for any 24-hour day desired

23. Of the following, the cleaning assignment which you would LEAST prefer to have per-   23.___
formed *during* school hours is

    A. sweeping of corridors and stairs
    B. cleaning and polishing brass fixtures
    C. cleaning toilets
    D. dusting of offices, halls and special rooms

24. A mechanical system of ventilation commonly found in schools is a unit ventilator   24.___
(univent) located in each classroom. Of the following, the procedure which is NOT usually correct with respect to operation and maintenance of this unit is

    A. air pressure for operation of the unit is obtained from a central fan located in the
       basement
    B. when a room is to be heated in the early morning of a cold day by recirculation, the
       window is closed and the damper opened to the room
    C. filters coated with oil are periodically cleaned by dipping them in a solution of wash-
       ing soda and hot water
    D. other radiators in the room are not normally controlled by the univent or its radiator

25. A teacher complains to you that her room is not cleaned properly each day. You have   25.___
received complaints from this teacher on several occasions and have found them to be
unfounded each time. The *most desirable* action to take is to FIRST

    A. tell the teacher that her room is cleaned as well as other rooms
    B. advise the teacher that she is expecting too much of the custodial staff
    C. ask the cleaner if he cleans that classroom in accordance with standard proce-
       dures
    D. visit the room to verify the complaint of the teacher

KEY (CORRECT ANSWERS)

1.	B		11.	C
2.	A		12.	A
3.	A		13.	B
4.	D		14.	B
5.	D		15.	D
6.	D		16.	B
7.	C		17.	B
8.	B		18.	C
9.	A		19.	C
10.	C		20.	A

21. A
22. A
23. D
24. A
25. D

EXAMINATION SECTION
TEST 1

DIRECTIONS: Each question or incomplete statement is followed by several suggested answers or completions. Select the one that BEST answers the question or completes the statement. *PRINT THE LETTER OF THE CORRECT ANSWER IN THE SPACE AT THE RIGHT.*

1. The pipe fitting that would be used to connect a 2" pipe at a 45° angle to another 2" pipe is called a(n)
   A. tee   B. orifice flange
   C. reducer   D. elbow

   1.___

2. An instrument that measures relative humidity is called a(n)
   A. manometer   B. interferemeter
   C. hygrometer   D. petrometer

   2.___

3. The one of the following flat drive-belts that gives the BEST service in dry places is a(n) _____ belt.
   A. rawhide   B. oak-tanned
   C. chrome-tanned   D. semirawhide

   3.___

4. The letter representing the standard V-belt section which has the LOWEST horsepower-per-belt rating is
   A. E   B. C   C. B   D. A

   4.___

5. A 6 x 19 wire rope has
   A. 6 strands
   B. 6 wires in each strand
   C. 19 strands
   D. 25 strands arranged in a 6 x 19 pattern

   5.___

6. A water tank 5 feet in diameter and 30 feet high has a volume of MOST NEARLY _____ cubic feet.
   A. 150   B. 250   C. 600   D. 1200

   6.___

7. The circumference of a circle with a radius of 5 inches is MOST NEARLY _____ inches.
   A. 31.3   B. 30.0   C. 20.1   D. 13.4

   7.___

8. A flexible coupling should be used to connect two shafts that
   A. have centerlines at right angles to each other
   B. may be slightly out of line
   C. start and stop too fast
   D. have different speeds

   8.___

9. Of the following materials used to make pipe, the one that is MOST brittle is
   A. lead   B. aluminum   C. copper   D. cast iron

   9.___

10. Mechanical equipment is generally tested and inspected   10.__
    on regular schedules in order to
       A. avoid breakdowns
       B. train new personnel
       C. maintain inventory
       D. give employees something to do

11. The *united inches* for a pane of glass that measures   11.__
    14 inches by 20 inches is
       A. 14   B. 34   C. 40   D. 54

12. The one of the following that should NOT be lubricated   12.__
    is a(n)
       A. spur gear train   B. motor commutator
       C. roller chain drive   D. automobile axle

13. One of the following oils that has the LOWEST viscosity   13.__
    is S.A.E.
       A. 70   B. 50   C. 20   D. 10W

14. A neoprene gasket would normally be used in a pipeline   14.__
    carrying
       A. steam   B. compressed air
       C. carbon dioxide   D. light oil

15. The one of the following that would NOT be used in   15.__
    cleaning toilet bowls is
       A. a cleaning cloth   B. oxalic acid
       C. muriatic acid   D. a detergent

16. An electric motor driven air compressor is automatically   16.__
    started and stopped by a
       A. thermostat   B. line air valve
       C. pressure switch   D. float trap

17. The term *kilowatt hours* describes the consumption of   17.__
       A. energy   B. radiation
       C. cooling capacity   D. conductance

18. AC voltage may be converted to DC voltage by means of a   18.__
       A. magnet   B. rectifier
       C. voltage regulator   D. transducer

19. When replacing a blown fuse, it is BEST to   19.__
       A. install another one of slightly larger size
       B. seek the cause of the fuse failure before replacing
          it
       C. install another one of size smaller
       D. read the electric meters as a check on the condition
          of the circuit

20. A 208 volt, 3 phase, 4 wire circuit power supply has a   20.__
    line to grounded neutral voltage of APPROXIMATELY _____
    volts.
       A. 120   B. 208   C. 220   D. 240

21. An interlock is generally installed on electronic equip-   21.___
    ment to
    A. prevent loss of power
    B. maintain VHF frequencies
    C. keep the vacuum tubes lit
    D. prevent electric shock during maintenance operations

22. A flame should not be used to inspect the electrolyte   22.___
    level in a lead-acid battery because the battery cells
    give off highly flammable
    A. hydrogen   B. lead oxide
    C. lithium   D. xenon

23. The purpose of the third prong in a three-prong male   23.___
    electric plug used in a 120 volt circuit is to
    A. make a firm connection   B. strengthen the plug
    C. ground to prevent shock   D. act as a transducer

24. A school custodian engineer on duty is informed that an   24.___
    employee under his supervision has just been injured in
    the school building.
    The FIRST course of action he should take is to
    A. inform his superior
    B. aid the injured employee
    C. call a meeting of all the men
    D. order an investigation

25. In the prevention of accidental injuries, the MOST   25.___
    effective procedure is to
    A. install safety guards
    B. alert the workers to the hazards
    C. install lighting for easy sight
    D. eliminate the accident hazard

KEY (CORRECT ANSWERS)

1. D	11. B
2. C	12. B
3. B	13. D
4. D	14. D
5. A	15. C
6. C	16. C
7. A	17. A
8. B	18. B
9. D	19. B
10. A	20. A

21. D
22. A
23. C
24. B
25. D

TEST 2

DIRECTIONS: Each question or incomplete statement is followed by several suggested answers or completions. Select the one that BEST answers the question or completes the statement. *PRINT THE LETTER OF THE CORRECT ANSWER IN THE SPACE AT THE RIGHT*.

1. The one of the following practices that will INCREASE the possibility of school fires occurring is the
   A. using of understairs areas for storage of all kinds
   B. wiping of machinery shafts with lubricating oil
   C. ventilating of all storage spaces
   D. cleaning of lockers at frequent intervals

1.___

2. When evaluating a building for fire hazards, the MOST important considerations are the
   A. number of stories and the height of each story
   B. location in the neighborhood and the accessibility
   C. interior lighting and the furniture
   D. number of residents and the use of the building

2.___

3. The one of the following that is a basic safety requirement for operating a power mower is:
   A. Fill gasoline driven mower indoors
   B. Do not operate power mowers on wet grass
   C. Keep the motor running when you leave the mower unattended for only a short while
   D. Fill the tank while the engine is running

3.___

4. You observe a red truck making a fuel delivery to your school.
   The fuel being delivered is PROBABLY
   A. gasoline   B. #2 fuel oil
   C. #4 fuel oil   D. #5 fuel oil

4.___

5. The one of the following steps that is NOT taken when operating a carbon dioxide fire extinguisher is to
   A. carry the extinguisher to the fire and set it on the ground
   B. unhook the hose
   C. pull the pin in the valve wheel
   D. turn the valve and direct the gas to the top of the fire

5.___

6. The BEST course of action to take to settle a job-related dispute that has arisen among two of your employees is to
   A. bring them both together, listen to their arguments, and then make a decision
   B. tell the two employees individually to settle their dispute

6.___

    C. tell both employees to submit their dispute in
       writing to you and then make a decision
    D. listen to the argument of each one separately and
       then make a decision

7. A school custodian engineer accidentally discovers a bottle   7.___
   of whiskey in a staff member's desk.
   The BEST procedure for the custodian to follow is to
    A. verbally reprimand him and prefer departmental
       charges
    B. inform him that whiskey is not allowed in school
       buildings
    C. call a meeting of all the employees and tell them
       what you found
    D. do nothing, as you do not want to embarrass the person

8. A new employee under your supervision constantly reports   8.___
   late for work.
   The one of the following actions you should take FIRST
   is to
    A. admonish him in front of the other employees
    B. prefer charges against him
    C. transfer him to another school
    D. warn him that he must be on time

9. The one of the following procedures that is BEST to   9.___
   follow when it is necessary to reprimand a worker is to
    A. issue the same reprimand to all of your men
    B. avoid him so he won't feel bad
    C. speak to him privately about the matter
    D. tell him what he has done wrong immediately to teach
       the other employees a lesson

10. The LEAST important factor to consider when evaluating   10.___
   the work of an employee is
    A. his grade on his civil service test
    B. the quality of his work
    C. his resourcefulness
    D. his attendance record

11. The one of the following supervisory actions that a   11.___
   school custodian engineer should use LEAST often is:
    A. Make periodic reports to his superior about the work
       of his men
    B. Bring employees up on *charges* whenever they do any-
       thing wrong
    C. Listen to staff grievances
    D. Advise an employee concerning a personal problem

12. The MAIN supervisory responsibility of a school custodian   12.___
   engineer is to
    A. foster policies of the Board of Education and the
       parents' organizations
    B. do his job so well that the students and employees
       like him

C. make assignments to his employees
D. operate and maintain facilities in a safe and
   efficient manner

13. One of your employees verbally protests to you about your   13.__
    evaluation of his work.
    The BEST way to handle him is to
      A. advise him of your lengthy and qualified experience
      B. tell him that you do not care to talk about it
      C. explain to him how you arrived at your evaluation
      D. tell him that since all of the other employees are
         satisfied, he should withdraw his complaint

14. A school custodian engineer will BEST keep the morales of   14.__
    his men high by
      A. giving praise for well-done work
      B. assigning good workers the most work
      C. personally helping each man in all the details of
         the man's job
      D. allowing special privileges for good work

15. In training maintenance personnel under the supervision   15.__
    of a school custodian engineer, the one of the following
    that should be given LEAST consideration by the custodian
    is
      A. how the training is to be given
      B. who is to be trained
      C. when the training will be given
      D. how the school principal wants them to be trained

16. The BEST attitude for a school custodian engineer to   16.__
    follow in his dealings with the public is to
      A. offer aid and cooperation to the public whenever
         possible
      B. show authority so that the public knows the limits
         to which they may make requests
      C. ignore the public, since the custodian has a specific
         job to do
      D. refer the public to a higher authority for solution
         of all their problems

17. The students playing in the schoolyard consistently lose   17.__
    rubber balls that land on the school roof. They request
    that you, the school custodian engineer, retrieve these
    balls.
    Of the following, the BEST procedure for you to follow is:
      A. Teach them a lesson and refuse to retrieve the balls
      B. Retrieve the balls and throw them into the incinera-
         tor
      C. One day a week retrieve the balls and return them
         to the students
      D. Retrieve the balls and give them to a local children's
         charity

18. The president of a charitable organization requests a   18.___
    permit to use the school building. You, the school
    custodian engineer, note that his same organization
    used the school previously and did not observe the *NO*
    SMOKING rules.
    The BEST procedure for you to follow is to
    A. deny the organization a permit since they did not
       obey the school regulations before
    B. issue the permit without any questions since a
       large group is difficult to control
    C. inform the president that if any of his members
       continue to disregard the no smoking rules, future
       permits will not be issued
    D. inform the president that if any of his members
       continue to disregard the no smoking rules, you will
       evict them from the school building

19. Due to some grievances, parents occupy your school on a   19.___
    weekend and refuse to leave.
    As the school principal is out of town and unavailable,
    the BEST procedure for you, the school custodian engineer
    on duty, is to
    A. tell your employees to vacate the school
    B. call the police department
    C. cooperate with the parents on the takeover
    D. lock all the people in the school

20. An organization requests a permit to use the school   20.___
    auditorium from the hours of 7 PM to 10 PM on a Tuesday
    evening. The organization also requests that its members
    be allowed to enter the school earlier than 7 PM and
    leave later than 10 PM.
    The BEST procedure for you, the school custodian engineer,
    to follow is to
    A. inform the organization leader that the organization
       may only use the school from the hours of 7 PM to
       10 PM
    B. issue the permit without saying anything as you want
       to maintain good public relations
    C. refer the matter to the school principal as you do
       not want to get involved
    D. ask the organization leader the reasons for the
       request and if the request is fair, issue the permit
       and let the organization do as it pleases

21. Dog owners in the neighborhood have been disregarding the   21.___
    Curb Your Dog signs and walking their dogs on your school
    lawn. You find that this interferes with the operation of
    powered lawn mowing equipment.
    Your BEST procedure to follow is to
    A. put up a higher fence
    B. chase the people and dogs away
    C. tell the owners you will call the police department
    D. explain the problem to the owners and ask them to
       curb their dogs

22. A cleaner reports to the school custodian engineer that
    a particular school room is consistently messy and dirty.
    The one who is equally at fault as the students for this
    dirty room is the
    A. students' parents
    B. regular classroom teacher
    C. student peer group
    D. cleaner for reporting the matter   22.___

23. A parent walks into a school custodian's office and starts
    to shout at him about a claimed injustice to her child.
    The PROPER procedure for the school custodian to follow
    is:
    A. Call the police department
    B. Summon the security guards
    C. Vacate the office
    D. Escort the parent to a guidance counselor   23.___

24. A newspaper reporter visiting a school should NORMALLY be
    referred to the
    A. school principal
    B. school custodian
    C. assistant superintendent of schools
    D. borough supervisor of school custodians   24.___

25. The parents of children in the neighborhood of your school
    complain to you that their children cannot use the school
    playground after school hours because the gates are closed.
    The BEST procedure for you to follow is to
    A. tell the parents the gates will remain closed after
       school hours
    B. arrange for the children to use a play street
    C. tell the parents to meet with the Board of Education
       on this matter
    D. try to arrange for the school gates to be open to a
       later hour after school hours   25.___

_____

KEY (CORRECT ANSWERS)

1. A		11. B
2. D		12. D
3. B		13. C
4. A		14. A
5. D		15. D
6. A		16. A
7. B		17. C
8. D		18. C
9. C		19. B
10. A		20. A

21. D
22. B
23. D
24. A
25. D

_____

EXAMINATION SECTION
TEST 1

DIRECTIONS: Each question or incomplete statement is followed by several suggested answers or completions. Select the one that BEST answers the question or completes the statement. *PRINT THE LETTER OF THE CORRECT ANSWER IN THE SPACE AT THE RIGHT.*

1. The one of the following devices that is required on BOTH coal-fired and oil-fired boilers is a(n)   1._____

   A. safety valve
   C. feed water regulator
   B. low water cut-off
   D. electrostatic precipitator

2. Lowering the thermostat setting by 5 degrees during the heating season will result in a fuel saving of MOST NEARLY _____ percent.   2._____

   A. 2   B. 5   C. 20   D. 50

3. An electrically-driven rotary fuel oil pump must be protected from internal damage by the installation in the oil line of a   3._____

   A. discharge-side strainer
   C. suction gauge
   B. check valve
   D. pressure relief valve

4. A float-thermostatic steam trap in a condensate return line that is operating properly will allow _____ to pass and will hold back _____.   4._____

   A. steam and air; condensate
   B. air and condensate; steam
   C. steam and condensate; air
   D. steam; air and condensate

5. Changes in the combustion efficiency of a boiler can be determined by comparing changes in stack temperature and   5._____

   A. steam pressure in the header
   B. over-the-fire draft
   C. percentage of carbon dioxide
   D. equivalent direct radiation

6. The classification of the coal that is USUALLY burned in school buildings is   6._____

   A. anthracite
   C. semi-bituminous
   B. bituminous
   D. lignite

7. A boiler is equipped with the following pressurtrols:
   I. Manual-reset pressurtrol
   II. Modulating pressurtrol
   III. High-limit pressurtrol
   The CORRECT sequence in which these devices should be actuated by rising steam pressure is: 7._____

   A. I, II, III
   C. III, I, II
   B. II, III, I
   D. III, II, I

8. The temperature of the returning condensate in a low-pressure steam heating system is 195° F.
This temperature indicates that

    A. some radiator traps are defective
    B. some boiler tubes are leaking
    C. the boiler water level is too low
    D. there is a high vacuum in the return line

8.___

9. An over-the-fire draft gauge in a natural draft furnace is USUALLY read in

    A. feet per minute   B. pounds per square inch
    C. inches of mercury   D. inches of water

9.___

10. The equipment which is used to provide tempered fresh air to certain areas of a school building is a(n)

    A. exhaust fan   B. window fan
    C. fixed louvre   D. heating stack

10.___

11. A chemical FREQUENTLY used to melt ice on outdoor pavements is

    A. ammonia   B. soda
    C. carbon tetrachloride   D. calcium chloride

11.___

12. A herbicide is a chemical PRIMARILY used as a(n)

    A. disinfectant   B. fertilizer
    C. insect killer   D. weed killer

12.___

13. Established plants that continue to blossom year after year without reseeding are GENERALLY known as

    A. annuals   B. parasites
    C. perennials   D. symbiotics

13.___

14. A ferrous sulfate solution is sometimes used to treat shrubs or trees that have a deficiency of

    A. boron   B. copper   C. iron   D. zinc

14.___

15. A tree is described as deciduous. This means PRIMARILY that it

    A. bears nuts instead of fruit
    B. has been pruned recently
    C. usually grows in swampy ground
    D. loses its leaves in the fall

15.___

16. If you are told that a container holds a 20-7-7 fertilizer, it is MOST likely that twenty percent of this fertilizer is

    A. nitrogen   B. oxygen
    C. phosphoric acid   D. potash

16.___

17. The landscape drawings for a school indicate the planting of <u>Acer platanoides</u> at a certain location on the grounds. Acer platanoides is a type of

    A. privet hedge   B. rose bush
    C. maple tree   D. tulip bed

17.____

18. A cleaner is attempting to lift a heavy drum of liquid cleaner from the floor to a shelf at waist height.
He is MOST likely to avoid personal injury in lifting the drum if he

    A. keeps his back as straight as possible and lifts the weight primarily with his back muscles
    B. arches his back and lifts the weight primarily with his back muscles
    C. keeps his back as straight as possible and lifts the weight primarily with his leg muscles
    D. arches his back and lifts the weight primarily with his leg muscles

18.____

19. Of the following, the BEST first aid treatment for a cleaner who has burned his hand with dry caustic lye crystals is to

    A. wash his hand with large quantities of warm water
    B. brush his hand lightly with a soft, clean brush and wrap it in a clean rag
    C. place his hand in a mild solution of ammonia and cool water
    D. wash his hand with large quantities of cold water

19.____

20. The purpose of the third prong in a three-prong electric plug used on a 120-volt electric vacuum cleaner is to prevent

    A. serious overheating of the vacuum cleaner
    B. electric shock to the operator of the vacuum cleaner
    C. generation of dangerous microwaves by the vacuum cleaner
    D. sparking in the electric outlet caused by a loose electric plug

20.____

21. Of the following, the LEAST effective method for a school custodian to use to reduce window glass breakage in his school is to

    A. keep the area near the school free of sticks and stones
    B. consult with parents and civic organizations and request their assistance in reducing breakage
    C. request that neighbors living near the school report after-hours incidents to the police department
    D. develop a reputation as a *tough guy* with the students so that they will be afraid to break windows in the school

21.____

22. The one of the following procedures that a school custodian should use when a telephone caller makes a threat to place a bomb in the school building is to

    A. hang up on the caller
    B. keep the caller talking as long as possible and make notes on what he says
    C. tell the caller he has the wrong number
    D. tell the caller his voice is being recorded and the call is being traced to its source

22.____

23. A school custodian is responsible for enforcing certain safety regulations in the school. 23.___
The MOST important reason for enforcing safety regulations is that

    A. every accident can be prevented
    B. compliance with safety regulations will make all other safety efforts unnecessary
    C. safety regulations are the law, and law enforcement is an end in itself
    D. safety regulations are based on reason and experience with the best methods of accident prevention

24. The safety belts that are worn by cleaners when washing outside windows should be 24.___
inspected

    A. before each use   B. weekly
    C. monthly   D. semi-annually

25. The one of the following actions that a school custodian should take to help reduce bur- 25.___
glary losses in the school is to

    A. leave all the lights on in the school overnight
    B. see that interior and exterior doors are securely locked at the end of the day
    C. set booby traps that will severely injure anyone breaking in
    D. set up an apartment in the school basement and stay at the school every night

————

KEY (CORRECT ANSWERS)

1.	A	11.	D
2.	C	12.	D
3.	D	13.	C
4.	B	14.	C
5.	C	15.	D
6.	A	16.	A
7.	B	17.	C
8.	A	18.	C
9.	D	19.	D
10.	D	20.	B

21.	D
22.	B
23.	D
24.	A
25.	B

————

EXAMINATION SECTION
TEST 1

DIRECTIONS: Each question or incomplete statement is followed by several suggested answers or completions. Select the one that BEST answers the question or completes the statement. *PRINT THE LETTER OF THE CORRECT ANSWER IN THE SPACE AT THE RIGHT.*

1. In city schools, wiring for motors or lighting is   1.____

    A. 208-220 volt, 4 wire, 60 cycle
    B. 240-110 volt, 3 wire, 4 phase
    C. 120-208 volt, 3 phase, 4 wire
    D. 160-210 volt, 4 phase, 3 wire

2. The LEAST likely cause of continuous vibration in a motor-driven pump is   2.____

    A. misalignment of motor and pump
    B. loose bearings in motor
    C. poor electric connection
    D. lack of graphite lubrication

3. A starter for fluorescent lights should be ordered in   3.____

    A. volts   B. amps   C. current   D. watts

4. A pipe is 50' long.   4.____
If it drops 1/4" each foot, how many inches does it drop in 50'?

    A. 5.5   B. 8   C. 10   D. 12.5

5. A plumber's friend operates by   5.____

    A. oscillation of water and air in the pipe
    B. density of water and pressure
    C. snake action
    D. water pressure *only*

6. Compound is applied to pipe thread.   6.____
When threading pipe, where would you apply compound?

    A. Male and female thread
    B. Female *only*
    C. Male *only*
    D. At the end of the male connection *only*

7. A 6/32 thread refers to   7.____

    A. stove bolt   B. pipe thread
    C. machine thread   D. drill bit

8. To hang a bulletin board on plaster or hollow tile wall, use   8.____

    A. self-tapping screws   B. wire cut nails
    C. expansion shields   D. molly shank and screw

9. To relieve the vacuum on a pump, one of the following should operate: 9.___

   A. discharge valve   B. vacuum breaker
   C. foot valve   D. bleeder valve

10. When water in circulating line shows brown, the LIKELY cause is   10.___

   A. bacteria build-up
   B. rust
   C. sluggish circulation
   D. water treatment plant excessive chemical build-up

11. The purpose of rear chamber in an incinerator is for   11.___

   A. arresting sparks   B. removing noxious gases
   C. smoke reduction   D. an extra source of O_2

12. A stack switch will shut down an oil burner when   12.___

   A. the temperature of the oil is low
   B. steam pressure is too high
   C. there is flame failure
   D. oil pressure is low

13. A check valve in a low pressure boiler water line is to   13.___

   A. prevent contamination of boiler water
   B. prevent return flow of water
   C. equalize boiler water level
   D. prevent the pressure from increasing

14. A custodian should know   14.___

   A. how to repair equipment
   B. condition before breakdown
   C. right lubrication to use
   D. outside conditions

15. In removing grass stains from marble and wood, which of the following should be used?   15.___

   A. Oxalic acid   B. Muriatic acid
   C. Sodium silicate   D. Disodium silicate

16. If concrete cracks appear in spring and winter, the cause is MOST likely   16.___

   A. poor concrete mix
   B. too much foot traffic
   C. poor sub-soil drainage
   D. not enough room for expansion and contraction

17. Venetian blinds should be cleaned by   17.___

   A. using feather duster
   B. vacuuming
   C. washing with clear water
   D. washing with cleaning solution

18. To keep chrome-plated metal clean, you should 18.____

    A. polish with fine steel wool
    B. wash with soapy water and polish with soft cloth
    C. clean with scouring powder and polish with soft cloth
    D. none of the above

19. After wetting down the floor with water solution, the BEST mop to use is 19.____

    A. a mop wet with clean water
    B. one wrung out in solution water
    C. a dry mop
    D. one wrung out in clear water

20. After sweeping and dusting a room, the LAST thing that should be done is 20.____

    A. empty waste basket   B. switch off lights
    C. close windows   D. clean the furniture

21. A preheater is used to heat # _____ oil. 21.____

    A. 1   B. 2   C. 4   D. 6

22. If paint blisters on the wall, the MOST likely cause is 22.____

    A. too much paint   B. porous plaster
    C. moisture in wall   D. hair-line plaster cracks

23. Cracks in newly plastered walls should be filled with 23.____

    A. putty   B. rough plaster first
    C. spackling plaster   D. silicone gel-fill

24. The BEST reason for cleaning light bulbs is 24.____

    A. the bulb will last longer
    B. removing dust
    C. obtaining optimum light
    D. preventing electrical shock

25. The color of fire lines is 25.____

    A. yellow   B. green   C. brown   D. red

26. To neutralize acid soil, which of the following should be used? 26.____

    A. Nitrogen   B. Potash
    C. Phosphorus   D. Lime

27. A cleaning detergent is composed of 27.____

    A. cleaning acids   B. salts
    C. sodium compounds   D. alkaline compounds

28. The BEST method to use in watering trees and shrubs is to use   28.___

    A. jet-type velocity at roots
    B. hose with fine nozzle spray once a week and done well
    C. a hose only when needed to soak roots
    D. rotating single jet sprinkler

29. As a custodian, which of the following instructions would you give your staff in case of   29.___
    fire?

    A. Report to Principal
    B. Go to location and put out fire
    C. Pull nearest fire alarm station box
    D. Make sure each one knows in advance their assigned location of duty when alarm
       rings

30. Which of the following effects does a foam extinguisher have?   30.___

    A. Smothering   B. Cooling and smothering
    C. Wetting down   D. Insulating

31. The BEST fire extinguisher to use on electric motors is   31.___

    A. soda acid   B. foam type
    C. carbon dioxide   D. water

32. Two employees are arguing about their personal clothing locker.   32.___
    How would you handle this dispute?

    A. Reprimand both men
    B. Talk to them individually
    C. Speak to both of them together about it
    D. Write up a disciplinary report on both men

33. A fertilizer 5-10-5 means   33.___

    A. 5 potash - 10 nitrogen - 5 phosphorous
    B. 5 tobacco chip - 10 potash - 5 phosphoric acid
    C. 5 tobacco chip - 10 nitrogen - 5 potash
    D. 5 potassium - 10 nitrogen - 5 phosphorous

34. Sand gravel mix should be   34.___

    A. 1 sand, 2 gravel, 3 cement
    B. 1 cement, 2 gravel, 3 sand
    C. 1 cement, 2 sand, 3 gravel
    D. 2 cement, 3 sand, 2 gravel

35. _____ is found between the boiler and boiler safety valve.   35.___

    A. Check valve   B. No valve
    C. Steam stop valve   D. Regulating valve

KEY (CORRECT ANSWERS)

1.	B		16.	D
2.	C		17.	A
3.	D		18.	B
4.	D		19.	C
5.	A		20.	B
6.	C		21.	D
7.	C		22.	C
8.	C		23.	B
9.	B		24.	C
10.	C		25.	D
11.	C		26.	D
12.	C		27.	C
13.	A		28.	C
14.	B		29.	D
15.	A		30.	B

31.	C
32.	B
33.	A
34.	C
35.	B

TEST 2

DIRECTIONS: Each question or incomplete statement is followed by several suggested answers or completions. Select the one that BEST answers the question or completes the statement. *PRINT THE LETTER OF THE CORRECT ANSWER IN THE SPACE AT THE RIGHT.*

1. Of the following, the BEST procedure in sweeping classroom floors is:

   A. Open all windows before beginning the sweeping operation
   B. The cleaner should move forward while sweeping
   C. Alternate pull and push strokes should be used
   D. Sweep under desks on both sides of an aisle while moving down the aisle

   1.___

2. Proper care of floor brushes includes

   A. washing brushes daily after each use with warm soap solution
   B. dipping brushes in kerosene periodically to remove dirt
   C. washing with warm soap solution at least once a month
   D. avoiding contact with soap or soda solutions to prevent drying of bristles

   2.___

3. An ADVANTAGE of vacuum cleaning rather than sweeping a floor with a floor brush is that

   A. stationary furniture will not be touched by the cleaning tool
   B. the problem of dust on furniture is reduced
   C. the initial cost of the apparatus is less than the cost of an equivalent number of floor brushes
   D. daily sweeping of rooms and corridors can be eliminated

   3.___

4. Sweeping compound for use on rubber tile, asphalt tile, or sealed wood floors must NOT contain

   A. sawdust   B. water
   C. oil soap   D. floor oil

   4.___

5. Of the following, the MOST desirable material to use in dusting furniture is a

   A. soft cotton cloth   B. hand towel
   C. counter brush   D. feather duster

   5.___

6. In high dusting of walls and ceiling, the CORRECT procedure is to

   A. begin with the lower walls and proceed up to the ceiling
   B. remove pictures and window shades only if they are dusty
   C. clean the windows thoroughly before dusting any other part of the room
   D. begin with the ceiling and then dust the walls

   6.___

7. When cleaning a classroom, the cleaner should

   A. dust desks before sweeping
   B. dust desks after sweeping
   C. open windows wide during the desk dusting process
   D. begin dusting at rows most distant from entrance door

   7.___

8. Too much water on asphalt tile is objectionable MAINLY because the tile   8._____

    A. will tend to become discolored or spotted
    B. may be loosened from the floor
    C. tends to disintegrate prematurely
    D. becomes too slippery to walk on

9. To reduce the slip hazard resulting from waxing linoleum, the MOST practical of the fol-   9._____
lowing methods is to

    A. apply the wax in one heavy coat
    B. apply the wax after varnishing the linoleum
    C. buff the wax surface thoroughly
    D. apply the wax in several thin coats

10. Assume that the water-emulsion wax needed for routine waxing in your building is 15 gal-   10._____
lons per month. This wax is supplied in 55 gallon drums.
To cover your needs for a year, the MINIMUM number of drums you should have to
request is

    A. two   B. three   C. four   D. six

11. In washing down walls, the correct procedure is to start at the bottom of the wall and   11._____
work to the top.
The MOST important reason for this is

    A. dirt streaking will tend to be avoided or easily removed
    B. less cleansing agent will be required
    C. rinse water will not be required
    D. the time for cleaning the wall is less than if washing started at the top of the wall

12. In mopping a wood floor of a classroom, the cleaner should   12._____

    A. mop against the grain of the wood wherever possible
    B. mop as large an area as possible at one time
    C. wet the floor before mopping with a cleaning agent
    D. mop only aisles and clear areas and use a scrub brush under desks and chairs

13. A precaution to observe in mopping asphalt file floors is: 13._____

    A. Keep all pails off such floors because they will leave water marks
    B. Do not wear rubber footwear while mopping these floors
    C. Use circular motion in rinsing and drying the floor to avoid streaking
    D. Never use a cleaning agent containing trisodium phosphate

14. The MOST commonly used cleansing agent for the removal of ink stains from a wood   14._____
floor is

    A. kerosene   B. oxalic acid
    C. lye   D. bicarbonate of soda

15. The FIRST operation in routine cleaning of toilets and wash rooms is to   15.___

    A. wash floors
    B. clean walls
    C. clean wash basins
    D. empty waste receptacles

16. To eliminate the cause of odors in toilet rooms, the tile floors should be mopped with   16.___

    A. a mild solution of soap and trisodium phosphate in water
    B. dilute lye solution followed by a hot water rinse
    C. dilute muriatic acid dissolved in hot water
    D. carbon tetrachloride dissolved in hot water

17. The principal reason why soap should NOT be used in cleaning windows is that   17.___

    A. it causes loosening of the putty
    B. it may cause rotting of the wood frame
    C. a film is left on, the window, requiring additional rinsing
    D. frequent use of soap will cause the glass to become permanently clouded

18. The CHIEF value of having windows consisting of many small panes of glass is   18.___

    A. the window is much stronger
    B. accident hazards are eliminated
    C. cost of replacing broken panes is low
    D. cleaning windows consisting of small panes is easier than cleaning a window with a large undivided pane

19. Cleansing powders such as Ajax should not be used to clean and polish brass MAINLY because   19.___

    A. the brass turns a much darker color
    B. such cleansers have no effect on tarnish
    C. the surface of the brass may become scratched
    D. too much fine dust is raised in the polishing process

20. To remove chalk marks on sidewalks and cemented playground areas, the MOST acceptable cleaning method is   20.___

    A. using a brush with warm water
    B. using a brush with warm water containing some kerosene
    C. hosing down such areas with water
    D. using a brush with a solution of muriatic acid in water

21. The MOST important reason for oiling wood floors is that   21.___

    A. it keeps the dust from rising during the sweeping process
    B. the need for daily sweeping of classroom floors is eliminated
    C. oiled floors present a better appearance than waxed floors
    D. the wood surface will become waterproof and stain-proof

22. After oil has been sprayed on a wood floor, the sprayer should be cleaned before storing   22._____
it.
The usual cleaning material for this purpose is

    A.   ammonia water   B.   salt
    C.   kerosene   D.   alcohol

23. The MOST desirable agent for routine cleaning of slate blackboards is   23._____

    A.   warm water containing trisodium phosphate
    B.   mild soap solution in warm water
    C.   kerosene in warm water
    D.   warm water alone

24. Neatsfoot oil is commonly used to   24._____

    A.   oil light machinery
    B.   prepare sweeping compound
    C.   clean metal fixtures
    D.   treat leather-covered chairs

25. Of the following daily jobs in the schedule of a custodian, the one he should do FIRST in   25._____
the morning is to

    A.   hang out the flag
    B.   open all doors of the school
    C.   fire boilers
    D.   dust the principal's office

26. When a school custodian is newly assigned to a building at the start of the school term,   26._____
his FIRST step should be to

    A.   examine the building to determine needed maintenance and repair
    B.   meet the principal and discuss plans for operation and maintenance of the building
    C.   call a meeting of the teaching and custodial staff to explain his plans for the build-
ing
    D.   review the records of maintenance and operation left by the previous custodian

27. A detergent is a material used GENERALLY for   27._____

    A.   coating floors to resist water
    B.   snow removal
    C.   insulation of steam and hot water lines
    D.   cleaning purposes

28. A good disinfectant is one that will   28._____

    A.   have a clean odor which will cover up disagreeable odors
    B.   destroy germs and create more sanitary conditions
    C.   diccolvo oncructod dirt and othor courcee of dieagreeable odors
    D.   dissolve grease and other materials that may cause stoppages in toilet waste lines

29. To help prevent leaks at the joints of water lines, the pipe threads are commonly covered   29.___
with

    A. tar   B. cup grease
    C. rubber cement   D. white lead

30. The advantage of using screws instead of nails is that   30.___

    A. they have greater holding power
    B. they are available in a greater variety than are nails
    C. a hammer is not required for joining wood members
    D. they are less expensive

31. Of the following, the grade of steel wool that is the FINEST is   31.___

    A. 00   B. 0   C. 1   D. 2

32. The material used with solder to make it stick better is   32.___

    A. oakum   B. lye   C. oil   D. flux

33. In using a floor brush in a corridor, a cleaner should be instructed to   33.___

    A. use moderately long pull strokes whenever possible
    B. make certain that there is no overlap on sweeping strokes
    C. give the brush a slight jerk after each stroke to free it of loose dirt
    D. keep the sweeping surface of the brush firmly flat on the floor to obtain maximum
        coverage

34. A device installed in a drainage system to prevent gases from flowing into a building is   34.___
called a

    A. trap   B. stall   C. cleanout   D. bidet

35. The plumbing fixture that contains a ball cock is the   35.___

    A. trap   B. water closet
    C. sprinkler   D. dishwasher

KEY (CORRECT ANSWERS)

1.	B	16.	A
2.	C	17.	C
3.	B	18.	C
4.	D	19.	C
5.	A	20.	A
6.	D	21.	A
7.	B	22.	C
8.	B	23.	D
9.	D	24.	D
10.	C	25.	C
11.	A	26.	B
12.	C	27.	D
13.	A	28.	B
14.	B	29.	D
15.	D	30.	A

31.	A
32.	D
33.	C
34.	A
35.	B

EXAMINATION SECTION
TEST 1

DIRECTIONS: Each question or incomplete statement is followed by several suggested answers or completions. Select the one that BEST answers the question or completes the statement. *PRINT THE LETTER OF THE CORRECT ANSWER IN THE SPACE AT THE RIGHT.*

1. In the wintertime, the FIRST thing a custodian does in the morning, after throwing the main switch, is to

   A. take a reading of the electric meter
   B. prepare his daily report of fuel consumption
   C. prepare sweeping compound
   D. inspect the water gauge of his boilers

   1._____

2. Rubbish, stones, sticks, and papers on lawns in front of school buildings are MOST effectively collected by means of a

   A. 30 inch floor brush with thickly set bristles
   B. corn broom
   C. 4 foot pole with a nail set in the bottom of it
   D. rake

   2._____

3. Which of the following statements about sweeping is NOT correct?

   A. Corridors and stairs should not be swept during school hours.
   B. Classrooms should usually be swept daily after the close of the afternoon session.
   C. Dry sweeping is not to be used in classrooms or corridors.
   D. Special rooms, as sewing rooms, may be swept during school hours if unoccupied.

   3._____

4. The PROPER size of floor brush to be used in classrooms with fixed seats is _____ inches.

   A. 36   B. 24   C. 16   D. 6

   4._____

5. Sweeping compound made of oiled sawdust should NOT be used on _____ floors.

   A. cement   B. rubber tile
   C. oiled wood   D. composition

   5._____

6. In oiling a wood floor, it is GOOD practice to

   A. apply the oil with a dipped mop up to the baseboards of the walls
   B. avoid application of oil closer than 6 inches of the baseboards
   C. keep the oil about one inch from the baseboard
   D. make sure that oil is applied to the floors under radiators

   6._____

7. Of the following, the LEAST desirable agent for cleaning blackboards is

   A damp cloth
   B. clear warm water applied with a sponge
   C. warm water with a little kerosene
   D. warm water containing a mild soap solution

   7._____

8. Chalk trays of blackboards should be washed and cleaned   8.___

    A. once a week
    B. daily
    C. only when the teacher reports cleaning needed
    D. once a month

9. In cleaning rooms by means of a central vacuum cleaning system,   9.___

    A. sweeping compound is used merely to prevent dust from rising
    B. rooms need cleaning only twice a week because the machine takes up the oil
    C. wood floors must be oiled more frequently as the machine takes up the oil
    D. the cleaner should not press down upon the tool but should guide it across the floor

10. A gas leak is suspected in the home economics class of a school. The procedure in locating the leak is to   10.___

    A. use a lighted match
    B. use a safety lamp
    C. place nose close to line and smell each section
    D. use soapsuds

11. The MOST important reason for placing asbestos jackets on steam lines is to   11.___

    A. prevent persons from burning their hands
    B. prevent heat loss
    C. protect the lines from injury
    D. make the lines appear more presentable

12. If the flag is used on a speaker's platform, it should be displayed   12.___

    A. above and behind the speaker
    B. as a drape over the front of the platform
    C. as a rosette over the speaker's head
    D. as a cover over the speaker's desk

13. When the flag of the United States of America is displayed from a staff projecting from the front of the building, it should be   13.___

    A. extended to the tip of the staff
    B. extended to about one foot from the tip of the staff
    C. secured so that there is a sag in the line
    D. extended slowly to the tip of the staff and then drawn back rapidly about 15 inches

14. The common soda-acid fire extinguisher should be checked and refilled   14.___

    A. every week   B. every month
    C. once a year   D. only if used

15. A small fire has broken out in an electric motor in a sump pump. The lubricant has apparently caught fire. The PROPER extinguisher to use is   15.___

    A. sand
    B. carbon tetrachloride (pyrene) fire extinguisher

C. soda-acid fire extinguisher
D. water under pressure from a hose

16. While cleaning windows, an employee falls from the fourth floor of the building to the sidewalk. The custodian finds the man unconscious.
The custodian should

    16._____

    A. move the man into a more comfortable position near the wall of the building and then call a doctor
    B. try to revive the man by depressing his head slightly and applying artificial respiration
    C. hail a taxi and bring the man to a hospital for treatment
    D. phone for an ambulance and cover the man to keep him warm

17. The duties of a custodian include the knowledge of safety rules to prevent accidents and injuries to his employees and himself.
Of the following, the LEAST harmful practice is to

    17._____

    A. carry a scraper in the pocket with the blade down
    B. measure the cleaning powder with your hands before placing the powder in water
    C. wet the hands before using steel wool
    D. use lye to clean paint brushes

18. The MOST important reason for not wringing out a mop by hand is that

    18._____

    A. water cannot be removed effectively in this way
    B. it is not fair to the cleaner
    C. the dirt remains on the mop after the water is removed
    D. pins, nails, or other sharp objects may be picked up and cut the hand, causing an infection

19. The method of using a ladder which you would consider LEAST safe is:

    19._____

    A. Grasping the side rails of the ladder instead of the rungs when going up
    B. To see that the door is secured wide open when working on a ladder at a door
    C. Leaning weight toward ladder while working on it
    D. Standing on top of the ladder to reach working place

20. When a window pane is broken, the FIRST step the custodian takes is to

    20._____

    A. remove broken glass from floors and window sill
    B. determine the cause
    C. remove the putty with a putty knife
    D. prepare a piece of glass to replace the broken pane

21. Your instructions to a cleaner about the proper sweeping of offices should include the following instruction:

    21._____

    A. Do not move chairs and wastebaskets from their places when sweeping
    B. Place chairs and baskets on the desks to get them out of the way
    C. Set aside the loose small furniture and chairs in an orderly manner when sweeping office floors
    D. Move the desks and chairs to the side of the room close to the wall in order to sweep properly

22. To remove dirt accumulations after the completion of the sweeping task, brushes should be   22.___

    A. tapped on the floor in the normal sweeping position
    B. struck on the floor against the side of the block
    C. struck on the floor against the end of the block
    D. turned upside down and the handle tapped on the floor

23. To sweep rough cement floors in a basement, the BEST tool to use is a   23.___

    A. deck brush   B. new 30" floor brush
    C. corn broom   D. treated mop

24. When a floor is scrubbed, it is NOT correct to   24.___

    A. use a steady, even rotary motion
    B. rinse the floor with clean hot water
    C. have the mop strokes follow the boards when drying the floor
    D. wet the floor first by pouring several bucketsful of water on it

25. Flushing with a hose is MOST appropriate as a method of cleaning   25.___

    A. terrazzo floors of corridors
    B. untreated wood floors
    C. linoleum floors where not in frequent use
    D. cement floors

KEY (CORRECT ANSWERS)

1.	D		11.	B
2.	D		12.	A
3.	A		13.	A
4.	C		14.	C
5.	B		15.	B
6.	D		16.	D
7.	C		17.	A
8.	A		18.	D
9.	D		19.	D
10.	D		20.	A

21.	C
22.	A
23.	C
24.	D
25.	D

TEST 2

DIRECTIONS: Each question or incomplete statement is followed by several suggested answers or completions. Select the one that BEST answers the question or completes the statement. *PRINT THE LETTER OF THE CORRECT ANSWER IN THE SPACE AT THE RIGHT.*

Questions 1-5.

DIRECTIONS: Column I lists cleaning jobs. Column II lists cleansing agents and devices. Select the proper cleansing agent from Column II for each job in Column I. Place the letter of the cleansing agent selected in the space at the right corresponding to the number of the cleansing job.

COLUMN I   COLUMN II

1. Chewing gum   A. Muriatic acid   1._____
                               B. Broad bladed knife
2. Ink stains   C. Kerosene   2._____
                               D. Oxalic acid
3. Fingermarks on glass   E. Lye   3._____
                               F. Linseed oil
4. Rust stains on porcelain   4._____

5. Hardened dirt on porcelain   5._____

6. When the bristles of a floor brush have worn short, the brush should be   6._____

   A. thrown away and the handles saved
   B. saved and the brush used on rough cement floors
   C. saved and used for high dusting in classrooms
   D. saved and used for the weekly scrubbing of linoleum floors

7. Feather dusters should NOT be used because they   7._____

   A. take more time to use than other dusters
   B. cannot be cleaned
   C. do not take up the dust but merely move it from one place to another
   D. do not stir up the dust and streak the furniture with dust rails

8. Floors that are usually NOT waxed are those made of   8._____

   A. pine wood   B. mastic tile
   C. rubber tile   D. terrazzo

9. For sweeping under radiators and other inaccessible places, the MOST appropriate tool   9._____
   is the

   A. counter brush   B. dry mop
   C. feather duster   D. 16" floor brush

10. A cleansing agent that should NOT be used in the cleaning of windows is   10.___

    A. water containing fine pumice
    B. water containing a small amount of ammonia
    C. water containing a little kerosene
    D. a paste cleanser made from water and cleaning powder

11. The BEST way to dust desks is to use a   11.___

    A. circular motion with soft dry cloth that has been washed
    B. damp cloth, taking care not to disturb papers on the desk
    C. soft cloth, moistened with oil, using a back and forth motion
    D. back and forth motion with a soft dry cloth

12. Trisodium phosphate is a substance BEST used in   12.___

    A. washing kalsomined walls
    B. polishing of brass
    C. washing mastic tile floors
    D. clearing stoppages

13. Treated linoleum is PROPERLY cleaned by daily   13.___

    A. dusting with a treated mop
    B. sweeping with a floor brush
    C. mopping with a weak soap solution
    D. mopping after removal of dust with a floor brush

14. Of the following, the MOST proper use for chamois skin is   14.___

    A. drying of window glass after washing
    B. washing of window glass
    C. polishing of metal fixtures
    D. drying toilet bowls after washing

15. A squeegee is a tool which is used in   15.___

    A. clearing stoppages in waste lines
    B. the central vacuum cleaning system
    C. cleaning inside boiler surfaces
    D. drying windows after washing

16. Concrete and cement floors are usually painted a battleship gray color. The MOST important reason for painting the floor is   16.___

    A. to improve the appearance of the floor
    B. the paint prevents the absorption of too much water when the floor is mopped
    C. the paint makes the floor safer and less slippery
    D. the concrete becomes harder and will not settle

17. After a sweeping assignment is completed, floor brushes should be stored   17.___

    A. in the normal sweeping position, bristles resting on the floor
    B. by hanging the brushes on pegs or nails

    C.   by piling the brushes on each other carefully in a horizontal position
    D.   in a dry place after a daily washing

18.   Painted walls and ceilings should be brushed down   18.____

    A.   daily
    B.   weekly
    C.   every month, especially during the winter
    D.   two or three times a year

19.   If an asphalt tile floor becomes excessively dirty, the method of cleaning should include   19.____

    A.   the use of kerosene or benzine as a solvent
    B.   the use of a solution of modified laundry soda
    C.   sanding down the spotted areas with a sanding machine on the wet floor
    D.   use of a light oil and treated mop

20.   To remove light stains from marble walls, the BEST method is to   20.____

    A.   use steel wool and a scouring powder, then rinse with clear warm water
    B.   wash the stained area with a dilute acid solution
    C.   sand down the spot first, then wash with mild soap solution
    D.   wet marble first, then scrub with mild soap solution using a soft fiber brush

21.   To rid a toilet room of objectionable odors, the PROPER method is to   21.____

    A.   spread some chloride of lime on the floor
    B.   place deodorizer cubes in a box hung on the wall
    C.   wash the floor with hot water containing a little kerosene
    D.   wash the floor with hot water into which some disinfectant has been poured

22.   Toilet rooms, to be cleaned properly, should be swept   22.____

    A.   daily
    B.   and mopped daily
    C.   daily and mopped twice a week
    D.   daily and mopped thoroughly at the end of the week

23.   In waxing a floor, it is usually BEST to   23.____

    A.   start the waxing under stationary furniture and then do the aisles
    B.   pour the wax on the floor, spreading it under the desks with a wax mop
    C.   remove the old wax coat before rewaxing
    D.   wet mop the floor after the second coat has dried to obtain a high polish

24.   The BEST reason why water should not be used to clean kalsomined walls of a boiler   24.____
    room is that the

    A.   walls are usually not smooth and will hold too much water
    B.   kalsomine coating does not hold dust
    C.   kalsomine coating will dissolve in water and leave streaks
    D.   wall brick and kalsomine coating will not dissolve in water and so cannot be
        cleaned

25. In mopping a floor, it is BEST practice to 25.___

    A. swing the mop from side to side, using the widest possible stroke across the floor up to the baseboard

    B. swing the mop from side to side, using the widest possible stroke across the floor surface, stopping the stroke from 3 to 5 inches from baseboards

    C. use short, straight strokes, up and back, stopping the strokes about 5 inches from the baseboards

    D. use short straight strokes, up and back, stopping the strokes at the baseboard

---

KEY (CORRECT ANSWERS)

1.	B		11.	D
2.	D		12.	C
3.	C		13.	A
4.	A		14.	A
5.	C		15.	D
6.	B		16.	B
7.	C		17.	B
8.	D		18.	D
9.	A		19.	D
10.	A		20.	D

21.	D
22.	B
23.	A
24.	C
25.	B

EXAMINATION SECTION
TEST 1

DIRECTIONS: Each question or incomplete statement is followed by several suggested answers or completions. Select the one that BEST answers the question or completes the statement. *PRINT THE LETTER OF THE CORRECT ANSWER IN THE SPACE AT THE RIGHT.*

1. The BEST of the following substances in which to store used paint brushes is

   A. gasoline
   C. alcohol
   B. mineral oil
   D. linseed oil

   1._____

2. A CORRECT statement with respect to the use of a file is:

   A. The coarser the tooth of a file, the less metal will be removed on each stroke of the file
   B. Files are generally made to cut in one direction only
   C. When a file is used to pry apart materials, light pressure should be maintained
   D. In filing rounded surfaces, the file should rest on the work at all times

   2._____

3. An ACCEPTABLE material to use on a door to overcome slight sticking to the door jamb is

   A. tallow candle
   C. mineral oil
   B. graphite
   D. #6 oil

   3._____

4. The PROPER type of wrench to use on plated or polished pipe is a(n) _____ wrench.

   A. monkey   B. pipe   C. open end   D. strap

   4._____

5. Of the following, the room which requires the GREATEST amount of illumination per square foot is the

   A. library
   C. auditorium
   B. gymnasium
   D. sewing room

   5._____

6. If one of the electric bulbs in a classroom fails to light up when the switch is snapped, the trouble is MOST likely with the

   A. switch   B. wiring   C. fuse   D. bulb

   6._____

7. In general, wood should be fine sanded _____ the grain.

   A. across
   C. with
   B. diagonal to
   D. circular to

   7._____

8. The reason for blowing down the water column of a boiler daily is to

   A. prevent priming or foaming in the boiler
   B. keep the passages above and below the glass clean
   C. remove lime and other mineral matter from boiler feedwater
   D. reduce the possibility of excess steam pressure from building up

   8._____

9. A CORRECT step in the procedure of blowing down a low pressure boiler is: 9.____

    A. Close return valves before starting to open the blow-off valve
    B. Start the job while the boiler is in operation
    C. Add fresh water rapidly to reach the maximum level
    D. Close blow-off valve when the water reaches the lowest row of tubes

10. To determine if efficient burning of fuel is occurring, the device which is used is a(n)   10.____

    A. orsat apparatus   B. thermostat
    C. pyrometer   D. bourdon tube

11. The PROPER tool to use to break up clinkers sticking to the grate is a   11.____

    A. shovel   B. slice bar
    C. grate bar   D. rake

12. One of the possible results of closing ash pit doors to regulate draft is   12.____

    A. warping or melting of grates
    B. reduced formation of clinkers
    C. steam will become superheated
    D. live coals will fall into the ash pit

13. Good firing methods require that   13.____

    A. the firebed be thick enough to prevent air from passing through
    B. each side of the grate be kept bare to allow cool air to reach the stack
    C. live coals should not be allowed to burn beneath the grates
    D. the fire be stirred every hour to reduce the amount of unburned gases

14. Of the following, the one that is CORRECT with respect to the burning of hard coal is: 14.____

    A. To prevent clinkers, a hard coal fire should never be poked
    B. The fire bed should not be more than 6 inches thick at any time
    C. Air holes in the bed should be made with a rake or slice bar
    D. Infrequent heavy firing will reduce the possibility of forming holes

15. The MAIN purpose of a Hartford Loop as a return connection for a steam boiler is to   15.____

    A. remove air from the return lines
    B. prevent a boiler from losing its water
    C. allow reduction in boiler header size
    D. reduce friction in return lines

16. If a boiler fails to deliver enough heat, the MOST probable of the following reasons is the   16.____

    A. leaking of the boiler manhole
    B. boiler operating at excessive output
    C. heating surface is covered with soot
    D. unsteady water line as shown by the gauge glass

17. Generally, thermostatic traps of radiators are used to   17.____

    A. prevent the flow of water and air and allow the passage of steam
    B. prevent the passage of steam and allow the passage of water and air

C. stop air from entering the radiator to prevent it from becoming air-bound
D. relieve the radiator of excess steam if pressure rises too high

18. When a heating boiler is in operation, the safety valve should be tested   18._____

    A. semi-annually
    B. weekly
    C. monthly
    D. whenever it seems to be stuck

19. In the horizontal rotary cup oil burner, the MAIN purpose of the rotary cup is to   19._____

    A. provide air for ignition of the oil
    B. pump oil into the burner
    C. atomize the oil into small drops
    D. turn the flame in a circle to heat the furnace walls evenly

20. The BEST reason for having gaskets on manholes of a boiler is to   20._____

    A. prevent leakage from the boiler
    B. provide emergency exit for excessive steam pressure
    C. provide easy access to the boiler for cleaning
    D. prevent corrosion at manholes

21. The MAIN purpose of expansion joints in steam lines is to   21._____

    A. provide for changes in length of heated pipe
    B. allow for connection of additional radiators
    C. provide locations for valves
    D. reduce breakage of pipe due to minor movement in the building

22. If too much water is put in a boiler, the result will be   22._____

    A. excessive smoke
    B. excessive rate of steam output
    C. excessive fuel consumption
    D. unsteady water line

23. Piping that carries condensate and air from radiators of a heating system is called   23._____

    A. dry return if above boiler water line
    B. drip line
    C. wet return if above boiler water line
    D. riser runout

24. Suppose a boiler smokes through the fire door.   24._____
    Of the following, the LEAST likely cause is

    A. dirty or clogged flues
    B. inferior fuel
    C. defective chimney draft
    D. air leaks into boiler

25. Of the following, the statement concerning accident prevention that is NOT correct is: 25.___

    A. Ladders should be unpainted
    B. Remove finger rings before beginning to mop
    C. Wear loose-fitting clothes when working around boilers or machinery
    D. Set ladder bottom at about 1/5 the ladder length away from the wall against which the ladder rests

---

KEY (CORRECT ANSWERS)

1.	D		11.	B
2.	B		12.	A
3.	A		13.	C
4.	D		14.	A
5.	D		15.	B
6.	D		16.	C
7.	C		17.	B
8.	B		18.	B
9.	B		19.	C
10.	A		20.	A

21.	A
22.	C
23.	A
24.	D
25.	C

TEST 2

DIRECTIONS: Each question or incomplete statement is followed by several suggested answers or completions. Select the one that BEST answers the question or completes the statement. *PRINT THE LETTER OF THE CORRECT ANSWER IN THE SPACE AT THE RIGHT.*

1. When the oil burner reset button is pressed, the burner motor does not start. The FIRST thing to check is the

    A. oil supply in oil tanks
    B. possibility of a blown fuse
    C. oil strainers which may be clogged
    D. dirty stack switch

1._____

2. When a heating plant is laid up for the summer, one of the steps the fireman should take with respect to the boiler is to tap the brace and stay rods with a hammer. The MAIN reason for this is to

    A. clean these parts of accumulated rust and dirt
    B. make certain these parts are in place and not out of line
    C. remove them for storage during summer and early autumn seasons
    D. make certain they are tight and not broken

2._____

3. In the event of a bomb threat, the custodian should take the precaution to

    A. open ash pit and fire doors of boilers
    B. pull the main switch to cut off all power in the building
    C. operate with the least number of water services possible
    D. empty water from boilers immediately after covering fire with ashes

3._____

4. The type of fire extinguisher that requires protection against freezing is

    A. carbon dioxide
    B. carbon tetrachloride (pyrene)
    C. soda acid
    D. calcium chloride

4._____

5. A CORRECT procedure in recharging soda acid fire extinguishers is:

    A. The soda charge should be completed dissolved in 28 gallons of boiling water
    B. The filled acid bottle should be tightly stoppered before it is placed back in the extinguisher
    C. The extinguisher must be recharged after use regardless of extent of use
    D. Be sure to fill container with soda solution to the top of container up to threads of cap

5._____

6. The MOST common cause of slipperiness of a terrazzo floor after being washed is the

    A. failure to rinse floor clean after cleaning agent is used
    B. destruction of floor seal by cleaning agent
    C. incomplete removal of dirt from the floor
    D. use of oil in the cleaning process

6._____

7. When electric lighting fixtures are washed, a precaution to observe is that 7.___

    A. the metal part of the fixture should be washed with a warm mild ammonia solution
    B. the holding screws of glass globes should be loosened about half a turn after cleaning globes
    C. trisodium phosphate should not be used in washing glass globes because it dulls glass
    D. chain links of fixture should be loosened to enable removal of entire fixture

8. Inside burns on recently cut pipe are USUALLY removed by 8.___

    A. filing   B. turning   C. reaming   D. sanding

9. When the average temperature for a day is 48°F, the number of degree days for that day is 9.___

    A. 22   B. 27   C. 12   D. 17

10. Water hammer will MOST likely occur in the 10.___

    A. self-closing valves of a drinking fountain
    B. bends in a pipe line where air can accumulate
    C. globe valve on the supply line to a fixture
    D. angle valve on the steam supply line to a radiator

11. To remove a stoppage in a trap which has not cleared by the use of a force cup, the tool to use is a(n) 11.___

    A. yarning tool   B. auger
    C. expansion bit   D. trowel

12. If the float of a flush tank leaks and fills with water, the MOST probable result will be 12.___

    A. no water in the tank
    B. ball cock remains open
    C. water will flow over the tank rim
    D. flush ball will not seat properly

13. Fresh air inlets are GENERALLY installed in connection with a 13.___

    A. house trap   B. roof vent
    C. sump pump   D. branch soil pipe

14. The PRIMARY function of the water trap in the waste line from a wash bowl is to 14.___

    A. hold excess water from flooding waste line
    B. prevent the flow of sewer gas into the room
    C. catch particles and refuse that may enter the line with the water
    D. provide an easy means for cleaning and repairing the waste line

15. The BEST lubricant for a cylinder lock is 15.___

    A. crude oil   B. machine oil
    C. tallow   D. graphite

16. A window sash holds the 16.___

    A. casing   B. glass   C. jambs   D. sills

17. The BEST procedure to follow to determine the actual cleaning ability of a specific material is to

    A. test its performance
    B. read the specifications
    C. ask the manufacturer
    D. examine trade literature

17.____

Questions 18-21.

DIRECTIONS: Questions 18 through 21 are to be answered on the basis of the following occurrence.

An accident occured at P.S. 947 on Monday, January 14, resulting in the injury of a fireman-cleaner named John Jones. Jones was found unconscious on the floor of the boiler room. He showed evidence of a head injury. An ambulance was called immediately. Jones was treated by the ambulance attendant, who found no serious injury and treated the head wound. Jones, when asked about the cause of the injury, stated that he had fallen over a coal shovel lying in his path. The head injury apparently resulted from the hard contact of Jones' head with a concrete post. Jones was then taken home and was advised to check with a doctor if he felt groggy or ill. An examination of the boiler room revealed that an electric light located near the scene of the accident was out and that the area was quite dark. There were no witnesses to the accident.

18. Of the following, the information MOST necessary to make the required report on the accident is

    A. Jones' age
    B. Jones' work habits
    C. the name of the person who found Jones injured
    D. whether Jones was covered by Workmen's Compensation

18.____

19. When Jones was found, a safety precaution that should have been taken was

    A. extinguishing the fire in the furnace
    B. the removal of Jones to a place where the lighting was more satisfactory
    C. avoiding movement of Jones to prevent further injury
    D. raising Jones' head to restore him to consciousness

19.____

20. In accordance with Worker's Compensation regulations, Jones has the right to

    A. compensation if his injuries keep him from work more than one week
    B. use any doctor provided the doctor is approved by the custodian
    C. compensation greater than the amount of his wages if he is seriously injured
    D. compensation only if he proves he did not place the shovel where it was found

20.____

21. The MOST important lesson that the custodian should learn from this accident is that

    A. before an employee starts work, his place of work should be inspected by the custodian
    B. even experienced firemen-cleaners require regular weekly training in the proper performance of their duties

21.____

C. employees should be required to turn in old burned out electric bulbs before receiving new ones
D. regular inspections of work spaces are required to reduce accidents to a minimum

22. Information which is of the LEAST value in a report of unlawful entry into a school building is the

22.____

A. estimated value of missing property
B. means of entry
C. time and date of entry
D. general description of the school building

23. You notice several children marking an entrance door with chalk. The MOST desirable immediate action to take is to

23.____

A. stop the children and tell them not to do this again
B. ask the principal to stop the children from defacing the door
C. take the names of the children and write to their parents
D. remove the chalk marks, but say nothing to the children

24. Suppose that the principal advises you that there are peddlers selling their wares at sidewalk locations surrounding the school premises.
The MOST appropriate action to take first is to

24.____

A. put up signs warning the peddlers that they are violating the law
B. advise the peddlers that such activity on sidewalks of the school is illegal and to move on
C. call the police immediately to clear the sidewalks
D. suggest that the teachers tell their pupils not to patronize these unsupervised peddlers

25. A parent complains that her child refuses to use the school toilet because it is unclean. The FIRST step you should take upon receipt of the complaint from the school principal is to

25.____

A. advise the principal that the toilets are kept clean and that the complaint is unwarranted
B. tell the cleaner in charge of the floor on which the toilet is located to clean the toilet properly
C. visit the school toilets to check on the statements made in the complaint
D. ask the parent to see the toilets for herself rather than take the word of her child

KEY (CORRECT ANSWERS)

1. B	11. B
2. D	12. B
3. C	13. A
4. C	14. B
5. C	15. D
6. A	16. B
7. B	17. A
8. C	18. C
9. D	19. C
10. A	20. A

21. D
22. D
23. A
24. B
25. C

EXAMINATION SECTION
TEST 1

DIRECTIONS: Each question or incomplete statement is followed by several suggested answers or completions. Select the one that BEST answers the question or completes the statement. *PRINT THE LETTER OF THE CORRECT ANSWER IN THE SPACE AT THE RIGHT.*

1. Of the following daily jobs in the schedule of a custodian, the one he should do FIRST in the morning is to

    A.   hang out the flag
    B.   open all doors of the school
    C.   fire the boilers
    D.   dust the principal's office

1.____

2. When a school custodian is newly assigned to a building at the start of the school term, his FIRST step should be to

    A.   examine the building to determine needed maintenance and repair
    B.   meet the principal and discuss plans for operation and maintenance of the building
    C.   call a meeting of the teaching and custodial staff to explain his plans for the building
    D.   review the records of maintenance and operation left by the previous custodian

2.____

3. A detergent is a material GENERALLY used for

    A.   coating floors to resist water
    B.   snow removal
    C.   insulation of steam and hot water lines
    D.   cleaning purposes

3.____

4. A good disinfectant is one that will

    A.   have a clean odor which will cover up disagreeable odors
    B.   destroy germs and create more sanitary conditions
    C.   dissolve encrusted dirt and other sources of disagreeable odors
    D.   dissolve grease and other materials that may cause stoppage in toilet waste lines

4.____

5. To help prevent leaks at the joints of water lines, the pipe threads are commonly covered with

    A.   tar   B.   cup grease
    C.   rubber cement   D.   white lead

5.____

6. The advantage of using screws instead of nails is that

    A.   they have greater holding power
    B.   they are available in a greater variety than are nails
    C.   a hammer is not required for joining wood members
    D.   they are less expensive

6.____

7. Of the following, the grade of steel wool that is FINEST is

    A.   00   B.   0   C.   1   D.   2

7.____

8. The material used with solder to make it stick better is   8.____

    A. oakum   B. lye   C. oil   D. flux

9. In using a floor brush in a corridor, a cleaner should be instructed to   9.____

    A. use moderately long pull strokes whenever possible
    B. make certain that there is no overlap on sweeping strokes
    C. give the brush a slight jerk after each stroke to free it of loose dirt
    D. keep the sweeping surface of the brush firmly flat on the floor to obtain maximum coverage

10. Of the following, the MOST proper procedure in sweeping classroom floors is to   10.____

    A. open all windows before beginning the sweeping operation
    B. move forward while sweeping
    C. alternate pull and push strokes
    D. sweep under desks on both sides of an aisle while moving down the aisle

11. PROPER care of floor brushes includes   11.____

    A. washing brushes daily after each use with warm soap solution
    B. dipping brushes in kerosene periodically to remove dirt
    C. washing with warm soap solution at least once a month
    D. avoiding contact with soap or soda solutions to prevent drying of bristles

12. An advantage of vacuum cleaning rather than sweeping a floor with a floor brush is that   12.____

    A. stationary furniture will not be touched by the cleaning tool
    B. the problem of dust on furniture is reduced
    C. the initial cost of the apparatus is less than the cost of an equivalent number of floor brushes
    D. daily sweeping of rooms and corridors can be eliminated

13. Sweeping compound for use on rubber tile, asphalt tile or sealed wood floors must NOT contain   13.____

    A. sawdust   B. water
    C. oil soap   D. floor oil

14. Of the following, the MOST desirable material to use in dusting furniture is a   14.____

    A. soft cotton cloth   B. hand towel
    C. counter brush   D. feather duster

15. In high dusting of walls and ceilings, the CORRECT procedure is to   15.____

    A. begin with the lower walls and proceed up to the ceiling
    B. remove pictures and window shades only if they are dusty
    C. clean the windows thoroughly before dusting any other part of the room
    D. begin with the ceiling and then dust the walls

16. When cleaning a classroom, the cleaner should   16.____

    A. dust desks before sweeping
    B. dust desks after sweeping

C. open windows during the desk dusting process
D. begin dusting at rows most distant from the entrance door

17. Too much water on asphalt tile is objectionable MAINLY because the tile   17.____

A. will tend to become discolored or spotted
B. may be loosened from the floor
C. will be softened and made uneven
D. colors will tend to run

18. To reduce the slip hazard resulting from waxing linoleum, the MOST practical of the fol-   18.____
lowing methods is to

A. apply the wax in one heavy coat
B. apply the wax after varnishing the linoleum
C. buff the wax surface thoroughly
D. apply the wax in several thin coats

19. Assume that the water-emulsion wax needed for routine waxing in your building is 15 gal-   19.____
lons per month. This wax is supplied in 55 gallon drums.
To cover your needs for a year, the MINIMUM number of drums you would have to
request is

A. two   B. three   C. four   D. six

20. In washing down walls, the correct procedure is to start at the bottom of the wall and   20.____
work to the top.
The MOST important reason for this is that

A. dirt streaking will tend to be avoided or easily removed
B. less cleansing agent will be required
C. rinse water will not be required
D. the time for cleaning the wall is less than if washing started at the top of the wall

21. In mopping a wood floor of a classroom, the cleaner should   21.____

A. mop against the grain of the wood wherever possible
B. mop as large an area as possible at one time
C. wet the floor before mopping with a cleaning agent
D. mop only aisles and clear areas and use a scrub brush under desks and chairs

22. A precaution to observe in mopping asphalt tile floors is: 22.____

A. Keep all pails off such floors because they will leave water marks
B. Do not wear rubber footwear while mopping those floors
C. Use circular motion in rinsing and drying the floor to avoid streaking
D. Never use a cleaning agent containing trisodium phosphate

23. The MOST commonly used cleansing agent for the removal of ink stains from a wood   23.____
floor is

A. kerosene   B. oxalic acid
C. lye   D. bicarbonate soda

24. The FIRST operation in routine cleaning of toilets and washrooms is to 24.____

    A. wash floors   B. clean walls
    C. clean washbasins   D. empty waste receptacles

25. To eliminate the cause of odors in toilet rooms, the tile floors should be mopped with 25.____

    A. a mild solution of soap and trisodium phosphate in water
    B. dilute lye solution followed by a hot water rinse
    C. dilute muriatic acid dissolved in hot water
    D. carbon tetrachloride dissolved in hot water

KEY (CORRECT ANSWERS)

1.	C	11.	C
2.	B	12.	B
3.	D	13.	D
4.	B	14.	A
5.	D	15.	D
6.	A	16.	B
7.	A	17.	B
8.	D	18.	D
9.	C	19.	C
10.	B	20.	A

21.	C
22.	A
23.	B
24.	D
25.	A

TEST 2

DIRECTIONS: Each question or incomplete statement is followed by several suggested answers or completions. Select the one that BEST answers the question or completes the statement. *PRINT THE LETTER OF THE CORRECT ANSWER IN THE SPACE AT THE RIGHT.*

1. The PRINCIPAL reason why soap should NOT be used in cleaning windows is that   1.____

   A.   it causes loosening of the putty
   B.   it may cause rotting of the wood frame
   C.   a film is left on the window, requiring additional rinsing
   D.   frequent use of soap will cause the glass to become permanently clouded

2. The CHIEF value of having windows consisting of many small panes of glass is that   2.____

   A.   the window is much stronger
   B.   accident hazards are eliminated
   C.   the cost of replacing broken panes is low
   D.   cleaning windows consisting of small panes is easier than cleaning a window with a large undivided pane

3. Cleansing powders such as Ajax should NOT be used to clean and polish brass MAINLY   3.____
   because

   A.   the brass turns a much darker color
   B.   such cleansers have no effect on tarnish
   C.   the surface of the brass may become scratched
   D.   too much fine dust is raised in the polishing process

4. To remove chalk marks on sidewalks and cemented playground areas, the MOST   4.____
   acceptable cleaning method is

   A.   using a brush with warm water
   B.   using a brush with warm water containing some kerosene
   C.   hosing down such areas with water
   D.   using a brush with a solution of muriatic acid in water

5. The MOST important reason for oiling wood floors is that   5.____

   A.   it keeps the dust from rising during the sweeping process
   B.   the need for daily sweeping of classroom floors is eliminated
   C.   oiled floors present a better appearance than waxed floors
   D.   the wood surface will become waterproof and stain-proof

6. After oil has been sprayed on a wood floor, the sprayer should be cleaned before storing   6.____
   it.
   The USUAL cleaning material for this purpose is

   A.   ammonia water   B.   salt
   C.   kerosene   D.   alcohol

7. The *MOST* desirable agent for routine cleaning of slate blackboards is 　　　　7.____

    A. warm water containing trisodium phosphate
    B. mild soap solution in warm water
    C. kerosene in warm water
    D. warm water alone

8. Neatsfoot oil is commonly used to 　　　　8.____

    A. oil light machinery
    B. prepare compound
    C. clean metal fixtures
    D. treat leather-covered chairs

Questions 9-12.

DIRECTIONS: Column I lists cleaning agents used by a custodian. Cleaning operations are given in Column II. Select the MOST common cleaning operation for the cleaning agents listed in Column I and print the letter representing your choice next to the number of the agent in the space at the right.

COLUMN I   COLUMN II

9. Ammonia   A. Add to water to clean marble walls   9.____

10. Muriatic acid   B. Remove chewing gum from wood floors   10.____

11. Carbon tetrachloride   C. Wash down calcimined ceilings   11.____

12. Trisodium phosphate   D. Add to water for washing rubber tile floors   12.____

                                 E. Remove rust stains from porcelain

                                 F. Cleaning brass

13. In order to stop a faucet from dripping, the custodian would USUALLY have to replace the 　　　　13.____

    A. cap nut   B. seat   C. washer   D. spindle

14. Drinking fountains should be adjusted so that the height of the water stream is about _____ inches. 　　　　14.____

    A. 6   B. 3   C. 0   D. 12

15. Before starting up the boilers each morning, the custodian or fireman should make certain that 　　　　15.____

    A. all blow-off cocks and valves are open
    B. the water is at a safe level
    C. radiator and univent valves are open
    D. the main smoke damper is fully closed

16. If the radiator on a one-pipe heating system rattles or makes noise, the PROBABLE cause is that the

    A. steam pressure is too high
    B. steam pressure is too low
    C. steam valve is wide open
    D. radiator is air-bound

16.____

17. Of the following, the LARGEST size of hard coal is

    A. chestnut   B. egg   C. stove   D. pea

17.____

18. The MAIN purpose of baffle plates in a furnace is to

    A. change the direction of flow of heated gases
    B. retard the burning of gases
    C. increase the combustion ratio of the fuel
    D. prevent the escape of flue gases through furnace openings

18.____

19. The MAIN difference between a steam header and a steam riser for a given heating system is that the

    A. riser is usually larger than the header
    B. header is larger than the riser
    C. riser is a horizontal line and the header is a vertical line
    D. header is insulated while the riser is not insulated

19.____

20. The try-cocks of steam boilers are used to

    A. act as safety valves
    B. empty the boiler of water
    C. test steam pressure in the boiler
    D. find the height of water in the boiler

20.____

21. The MOST important reason for cleaning soot from a boiler is that

    A. soot blocks the passage of steam from the boiler
    B. soot gets into the boiler room and makes it dirty
    C. soot reduces the heating efficiency of a boiler
    D. the pressure of soot is a frequent cause of the cracking of boiler tubes

21.____

22. Panic bolts are standard equipment in school buildings.
Their MAIN purpose is to

    A. reduce unauthorized opening of doors and closets
    B. allow for easy opening of exit doors of the building
    C. permit rapid removal of screens from windows when a fire occurs
    D. shut storeroom doors automatically to reduce fire hazard

22.____

23. The term RPM is GENERALLY used in connection with the

    A. speed of ventilating fans
    B. water capacity of pipe
    C. heating quality of fuel
    D. electrical output of a transformer

23.____

24. A hacksaw is a light-framed saw MOST commonly used to

    A. cut curved patterns in metal
    B. trim edges
    C. cut wood in confined spaces
    D. cut metal

24.____

25. A kilowatt is equivalent to _____ watts.

    A. 500   B. 2,000   C. 1,500   D. 1,000

25.____

KEY (CORRECT ANSWERS)

1.	C		11.	B
2.	C		12.	D
3.	C		13.	C
4.	A		14.	B
5.	A		15.	B
6.	C		16.	D
7.	D		17.	B
8.	D		18.	A
9.	A		19.	B
10.	E		20.	D

21.	C
22.	B
23.	A
24.	D
25.	D

EXAMINATION SECTION
TEST 1

DIRECTIONS: Each question or incomplete statement is followed by several suggested answers or completions. Select the one that BEST answers the question or completes the statement. *PRINT THE LETTER OF THE CORRECT ANSWER IN THE SPACE AT THE RIGHT.*

1. Of the following, the size of hard coal which is the SMALLEST is   1.____

    A. egg   B. stove   C. broken   D. buckwheat

2. If the CO_2 content of the flue gases of an oil burner is very high, it USUALLY indicates   2.____

    A. too much oil admitted to the furnace
    B. good combustion of fuel
    C. good circulation of steam
    D. excessive steam production

3. When a steam radiator in a one-pipe gravity system is air-bound, the cause is *most likely* to be   3.____

    A. defective air valve
    B. air entering through a leaking line
    C. insufficient steam pressure
    D. defective gate valve

4. Of the following, the one which is *most unlikely* to cause warping or burning of grate bars is   4.____

    A. leaving grates uneven after shaking
    B. allowing free passage of air through the bars
    C. accumulating ashes in the ashpit
    D. shaking all ashes through to the ashpit in an active furnace

5. A wet return is BEST defined as a   5.____

    A. return line below the level of water in the boiler
    B. return that contains water as well as steam
    C. return that has an improper pitch causing backing up of water
    D. gravity return from which air has been removed

6. The MAIN supply of air for the burning of fuel in a coal-fired boiler enters through the _____ damper.   6.____

    A. fire door   B. ashpit door
    C. breeching   D. check

7. Steam traps are devices which serve to   7.____

    A. by-pass steam flow where radiators are filled with steam
    B. shut down rate of steam flow when steam temperature is too high
    C. separate air and condensate from steam in steam heating systems
    D. prevent the development of high steam pressures by releasing excess steam

8. When the diaphragm or bellows of a thermostatic radiator trap is found to be dirty, it is USUALLY cleaned with   8._

    A. kerosene
    C. mild soap and water
    B. carbon tetrachloride
    D. turpentine

9. It is found that water is being carried over from an operating boiler into the steam main. Of the following, the one that is LEAST likely as the possible cause is   9._

    A. water level higher than specified for the boiler
    B. grease and dirt in the boiler
    C. excessive rate of output
    D. insufficient installed radiation

10. Of the following, the PROPER step to take when firing a boiler by the coking method is to   10._

    A. push the live coals to the rear of the grates and add fresh coal to the front part of the grates
    B. spread out the live coals and cover them frequently with a thin layer of fresh coal
    C. push the live coals to one side and place fresh coals on the other side, changing sides each time coal is added
    D. shovel the fresh coal on the rear of the grates and then cover them partly with live coals

11. Turpentine is added to paint MAINLY to   11._

    A. enable it to dry more rapidly
    B. dissolve the pigment in the paint
    C. add corrosion resisting properties to the paint
    D. thin out the paint

12. Automatic operation of a sump pump is controlled by the   12._

    A. electric switch
    C. foot valve
    B. float
    D. centrifugal driving unit

13. Kerosene costs 36 cents a quart. At that rate, two gallons would cost   13._

    A. $1.44   B. $2.16   C. $2.88   D. $3.60

14. A PROPER procedure in the event of fire in a school building is to   14._

    A. shut down all utilities - gas, electricity, and water
    B. maintain normal steam pressure in high pressure boilers equipped with auxiliaries driven by utility company electric power
    C. shut down all ventilating fans on central duct systems
    D. open all fire doors on the various floors to ventilate the fire

15. Piping used to carry electric wiring is COMMONLY called   15._

    A. conduit   B. leader   C. conductor   D. sleeve

16. The MAIN objection to using a copper penny in place of a blown fuse is that   16._

    A. the penny will conduct electric current
    B. the penny will reduce the current flowing in the line
    C. melting of the penny will probably occur
    D. the line will not be protected against excessive current

17. A rip saw is GENERALLY used to cut   17.____

    A. corners   B. uneven ragged lumber strips
    C. with the grain   D. across the grain

18. Sweating USUALLY occurs in pipes that   18.____

    A. contain hot water   B. contain cold water
    C. are chrome plated   D. require insulation

19. Workmen's Compensation insurance USUALLY provides   19.____

    A. employee benefits whether or not the injury was his fault
    B. employee benefits only if the employee was not negligent or exceptionally careless
    C. medical benefits in all cases, and compensation if no negligence or deliberate
        injury is found
    D. all benefits if absent from work four days or more

20. Of the following, the MOST important reason for making supply inventories is to   20.____

    A. schedule work assignments properly
    B. make certain that the supply room is in an orderly condition
    C. determine if employees are working efficiently
    D. check on the use of materials

21. Suppose that you are preparing a semi-annual requisition for janitorial supplies. The   21.____
    PROPER procedure in preparing the requisition is to

    A. order one and one-half times the amount actually needed to be sure of an ade-
        quate reserve
    B. order the amount actually needed as based on past use and probable needs
    C. ask each member of your staff to submit a statement of the supplies he will need
        for the next six months
    D. order 10% more than the previous year to cover all possible emergencies

22. Beginning of period   22.____

End of period

The amount of gas in cubic feet used during the measured period is
A. 183   B. 283   C. 362   D. 454

23. The MOST probable cause of foaming of a boiler that has been recently installed is   23.__

     A. poor draft
     B. higher than normal water level
     C. grease and oil in boiler
     D. excessive rate of output

24. When banking a fire, a PROPER step to take is to   24.__

     A. avoid any bright spots in the fuel bed
     B. close damper tightly
     C. open ashpit doors fully
     D. close fire doors

25. Of the following, the one which is considered poor practice in boiler operation is keeping   25.__

     A. valves at the top and bottom of the water gauge glass open whenever operating boiler
     B. steam gauge cock open at all times when boiler is in operation
     C. fuel bed as light and shallow as possible to maintain fuel economy
     D. a thin ash layer over the grate to protect the bars from heat

26. A PROPER procedure in boiler operation is to blow down   26.__

     A. boilers and condensate tanks weekly
     B. the water column daily
     C. the water column weekly
     D. boilers only when necessary

27. The MAIN purpose of a condensate pump is to   27.__

     A. return water from the return lines to a boiler
     B. pump make-up water to maintain water level
     C. maintain steam pressure in the supply lines
     D. provide for continuous draining of radiators under pressure

28. In an oil-fired plant, the emergency or remote control switch is USUALLY located   28.__

     A. at the entrance to the boiler room
     B. next to the oil burner
     C. at the panel board in the boiler room
     D. at the electrical distribution panel for the building

29. A safety device which is COMMONLY used in oil burner operation to detect flame failure   29.__
and shut down the burner is a

     A. thermostat   B. stackswitch
     C. aquastat   D. yulatrol

30. Of the following items, the one that has LEAST relation to the ignition system of an automatic horizontal rotary cup oil burner is a   30.____

    A. transformer   B. electrode
    C. gas valve   D. oil metering valve

31. The pressure of oil in the oil supply piping to a rotary cup oil burner is about 40 pounds.   31.____
    This pressure is maintained MAINLY in order to

    A. bring the oil into the atomizing cup
    B. mix the oil together with the primary air
    C. operate the magnetic oil valve
    D. avoid having the oil spray strike the edge of the oil nozzle

32. The atomizing cup of an oil burner shows carbon deposits. Of the following, the MOST   32.____
    desirable way to remove these deposits is to

    A. use a scraper, followed by light rubbing with 00 sandpaper
    B. wash the cup and nozzle with a mild trisodium phosphate solution and dry with a
       cloth
    C. use kerosene to loosen the deposits and wipe with a soft cloth
    D. apply a hot flame to the carbonized surfaces to burn off the carbon deposits

33. The MAJOR purpose of keeping the boiler filled with water during the non-heating sea-   33.____
    son is that

    A. corrosion of interior parts will be prevented
    B. leaks in the boiler or piping will be detected more easily before the heating season
       begins
    C. no time will be lost in filling the boiler when the heating season starts
    D. scale deposits and impurities in the water will be reduced to a minimum

34. A MAJOR disadvantage of self-closing faucets in lines operating under moderate water   34.____
    pressure is that they

    A. close too rapidly
    B. frequently produce water hammer
    C. open too easily
    D. tend to become filled with sediment

35. When lamps are wired in parallel, the failure of one lamp will   35.____

    A. break the electric circuit to the other lamps
    B. have no effect on the power supply to the other lamps
    C. increase noticeably the light production of the other lamps
    D. cause excessive current to flow through the other lamps

36. A cotter pin is used to   36.____

    A. set tile
    B. reduce bushings
    C. strengthen bolts to stand a greater pull
    D. keep a nut from working loose

37. Of the following valves, the one which is automatic in operation is 37._

    A. check   B. globe   C. angle   D. gate

38. The name of a fitting used to make a turn in the direction of a pipe line is 38._

    A. union   B. bushing   C. elbow   D. coupling

39. If the flush tank of a water-closet fixture overflows, the fault is likely to be 39._

    A. failure of the ball to seat properly
    B. excessive water pressure
    C. defective trap in the toilet bowl
    D. water-logged float

40. For the purpose of fire prevention, it is MOST important that the custodian 40._

    A. know how to attack fires whatever their size
    B. detect and eliminate every possible fire hazard
    C. train his staff to place inflammables in fireproof containers
    D. see that halls, corridors, and exits are not blocked

41. In addition to his utilitarian duties and responsibilities, the custodian shall have general 41._
responsibility to assist the educational system by developing the cultural function of envi-
ronment. This should follow automatically if his utilitarian work is well accomplished. This
statement means *most nearly* that

    A. the custodian must act as a teacher of school children as well as operating and
        maintaining his building in accordance with highest standards
    B. if a custodian observes a teacher neglecting to discipline children properly, it is his
        duty to correct this failure
    C. the custodian must train his staff just as the educational system teaches children
        so that both achieve a higher cultural level
    D. if a custodian operates and maintains his building properly, he will assist in
        enabling teachers to do a better job

42. When you hire a new employee and you are preparing to train him in the work he is to 42._
perform, the FIRST thing to do is to

    A. tell him what his job is and find out what he already knows about it
    B. prepare a written description of the tasks the employee is to do and have him study
        them
    C. make certain that the employee has all the proper tools and materials and knows
        how to store them
    D. have him work along with another older employee to learn the requirements of the
        job

43. A cleaner tells you that several teachers do not keep their rooms clean, resulting in extra 43._
work for him. Assuming that he is correct in his claim, the MOST desirable step to take is
to

    A. visit the teachers directly and ask them to manage their classes so as to avoid
        excessive cleaning
    B. suggest to the principal that he discuss this cleaning problem with his teaching
        staff
    C. advise the cleaner to discuss the matter with the teachers involved
    D. tell the cleaner that nothing can be done and that he'll just have to do the extra
        cleaning

44. When a repair is required in your school, the FIRST thing to do is to

    A. determine if you and your staff can handle it
    B. ask for assistance from the repair shop
    C. find out exactly what has to be done
    D. make a list of the materials and tools needed

44._____

45. A teacher complains to you that one of your staff failed to acknowledge his greeting and was not a very pleasant person. The MOST reasonable thing to do is to

    A. tell the teacher that the employee does his work well and that that is all you can ask of him
    B. advise the teacher to speak to the school principal if he has any real grievance
    C. tell the employee to be more polite to the teacher or he may lose his job
    D. discuss with your staff the need for a more friendly attitude toward the teaching staff

45._____

46. A cleaner asks to have his hours of work changed. You find that you cannot grant this request because you require coverage during those hours. Under the circumstances, you should

    A. tell the cleaner that you cannot grant his request because the main office frowns on schedule changes
    B. deny his request and give your reasons for such denial
    C. advise the cleaner that if you changed his hours, other employees might make similar requests
    D. tell the cleaner that he should try to find another job with hours suitable to his needs

46._____

47. The purpose of a safety valve on a steam boiler is to

    A. start the feed pump when the water is low
    B. dampen the fire when the boiler is overheated
    C. shut off the feed pump when enough water is let into the boiler
    D. release the steam when the pressure gets too great

47._____

48. A device which is LEAST likely to be found in low pressure heating plants is a(n)

    A. vacuum pump
    C. economizer
    B. inverted bucket trap
    D. Hartford return connection

48._____

49. Baffle plates are sometimes put into furnaces to

    A. change the direction of heated gases
    B. increase the combustion of the fuel
    C. retard the burning of the gases
    D. prevent overloading of the combustion chamber

49._____

50. An operating boiler explosion may be caused by 50._

    A. accumulation of gas in the furnace
    B. too deep a fire
    C. overpressure of steam
    D. too much water in the boiler

_____

KEY (CORRECT ANSWERS)

1. D	11. D	21. B	31. A	41. D
2. B	12. B	22. C	32. C	42. A
3. A	13. C	23. C	33. A	43. B
4. B	14. C	24. D	34. B	44. C
5. A	15. A	25. C	35. B	45. D
6. B	16. D	26. B	36. D	46. B
7. C	17. C	27. A	37. A	47. D
8. A	18. B	28. A	38. C	48. C
9. D	19. A	29. B	39. D	49. A
10. A	20. D	30. D	40. B	50. C

_____

TEST 2

DIRECTIONS: Each question consists of a statement. You are to indicate whether the statement is TRUE (T) or FALSE (F). *PRINT THE LETTER OF THE CORRECT ANSWER IN THE SPACE AT THE RIGHT.*

1. The amount of furniture in a classroom determines to a large extent the time that will be required to sweep it.   1._____

2. Exterior bronze should be wiped periodically with a soft cloth dampened with a light oil such as lemon oil   2._____

3. A gallon of kerosene is heavier than a gallon of water.   3._____

4. The purpose of boiler feedwater treatment compound added to boiler water is to eliminate minor leaks in the boiler shell.   4._____

5. Air pockets occur more frequently in one-pipe heating systems than in two-pipe systems.   5._____

6. Floor brushes should always be hung on pegs when not in use.   6._____

7. A floor brush, when used on a classroom floor, will stir up more dust than a good corn broom.   7._____

8. When sweeping a classroom with fixed desks and seats, the cleaner should use push strokes rather than pull strokes whenever possible.   8._____

9. Stick shellac is often used to fill in scratches and dents in furniture.   9._____

10. Although an ammonia solution is a good glass cleanser, it may darken the putty or painted frames of windows.   10._____

11. Chamois skins should be completely dry if they are to be used to dry windows or exterior glass.   11._____

12. The portable vacuum cleaner used in a school can be applied effectively to remove soot from boiler tubes.   12._____

13. If classroom floors are cleaned by means of a heavy-duty vacuum cleaner, they need not be cleaned daily.   13._____

14. Calcimined ceilings should be washed with lukewarm water occasionally to remove the accumulated dirt.   14._____

15. Corn brooms should be wet with warm water once or twice a week to keep the fibers flexible.   15._____

16. A good time to wash windows is when the sun is shining on them.   16._____

17. When a floor is to be mopped, the cleaner should plan to mop only small areas at a time.   17._____

18. When mopping, the mop stroke used should be wide enough so that the mop can touch the baseboards of the room.   18._____

19. Toilet room odors tend to become more noticeable as the temperature of the room goes down. 19.__

20. Sweeping of a toilet floor should usually start at the door entrance and end at the far corner of the room. 20.__

21. When a mopping job is finished, the floor should be practically dry. 21.__

22. Dirt should be cleaned out from behind radiators before a classroom or corridor is swept. 22.__

23. When grease is to be dissolved in a clogged drain, it is more desirable to use lye than caustic potash. 23.__

24. A purpose for which school classroom floors are oiled is to help preserve the wood. 24.__

25. It usually takes less time to sweep an oiled wood floor than an unoiled wood floor. 25.__

26. It is a good idea to soak new mop heads in boiling hot water for a short time before using them. 26.__

27. A desirable way to remove dry paint from glass is to use a very fine sandpaper. 27.__

28. A nail comb is commonly used to clean grease and dirt from the surfaces of nails. 28.__

29. A force cup or *plumbers friend* is used to remove obstructions in plumbing fixtures. 29.__

30. Panic bolts are usually found attached to swing-type window frames. 30.__

31. Good conductors of heat make good insulating material for covering hot water piping. 31.__

32. Slate blackboards in classrooms should usually be washed once a week. 32.__

33. A soda-acid fire extinguisher must be recharged after each use, no matter how slightly it has been used. 33.__

34. It is not practical to varnish wood floors in schools because the varnish coat is soon marred by heavy traffic. 34.__

35. A circular motion in washing and drying window glass is a more rapid and efficient method than a back-and-forth method. 35.__

36. The highest number visible on a steam gauge indicates the maximum allowable pressure in the boiler. 36.__

37. The outside doors of school buildings should open inward. 37.__

38. For interior building wiring, No. 14 wire is usually thicker than No. 12 wire. 38.__

39. Natural ventilation is obtained by adjusting the openings of windows and transoms. 39.__

40. Floor hair brushes should, in general, be kept dry because water tends to ruin them. 40.__

41. Wood floors should be mopped across the grain wherever possible. 41.__

42. Pails filled with cleaning solutions for mopping a floor should be placed on a wet space to prevent rings.   42.____

43. To effectively clean linoleum floors, very hot water should be used.   43.____

44. Cork tile requires a sealer coat before it is waxed for the first time.   44.____

45. The time it should take to dust the furniture of an average classroom each morning is about 5 or 6 minutes.   45.____

46. High dusting of classrooms should follow dusting of chairs, desks, and window sills.   46.____

47. Flathead screws should be countersunk into the material fastened.   47.____

48. The size of a nut is given by the diameter and number of threads per inch of the bolt it fits.   48.____

49. A good practice in boiler operation is to remove ashes from ashpits once a week during the heating season.   49.____

50. A transformer is a device used to raise or lower A.C. voltage.   50.____

KEY (CORRECT ANSWERS)

1.	T	11.	F	21.	T	31.	F	41.	F
2.	T	12.	T	22.	T	32.	T	42.	T
3.	F	13.	F	23.	F	33.	T	43.	F
4.	F	14.	F	24.	T	34.	T	44.	T
5.	F	15.	T	25.	T	35.	F	45.	T
6.	T	16.	F	26.	T	36.	F	46.	F
7.	F	17.	T	27.	F	37.	F	47.	T
8.	T	18.	F	28.	F	38.	F	48.	T
9.	T	19.	F	29.	T	39.	T	49.	F
10.	T	20.	F	30.	F	40.	T	50.	T

TEST 3

DIRECTIONS: Each question consists of a statement. You are to indicate whether the statement is TRUE (T) or FALSE (F). *PRINT THE LETTER OF THE CORRECT ANSWER IN THE SPACE AT THE RIGHT.*

1. White spots on waxed woodwork due to water or dampness may be removed with alcohol.　1.__

2. A counter brush should not be used to sweep under radiators or lockers.　2.__

3. A good way to dispose of waste paper in a school building is to burn the paper in the steam heating furnace.　3.__

4. Oxalic acid can be used to remove ink stains and rust from woodwork.　4.__

5. A desirable method of removing fingerprints and hardened dirt from porcelain fixtures is to apply a strong coarse powder cleanser.　5.__

6. Wet mop filler replacements are ordered by the weight of the filler, not the length of the strands.　6.__

7. A desirable method of controlling unpleasant odors in a washroom is to use pungent deodorants.　7.__

8. Fuses for branch lighting circuits are usually rated in watts.　8.__

9. The main purpose of oil in a bearing is to prevent the metal parts from touching.　9.__

10. Metal lighting fixtures should not be washed, but should be dusted and wiped lightly with a damp cloth.　10.__

11. The washing of painted walls should begin at the top and proceed down to the bottom of the wall.　11.__

12. Check valves are used to control the direction of flow of water or steam.　12.__

13. A blow-off valve on a boiler is used mainly to reduce steam pressure.　13.__

14. A wood floor should be slightly damp from washing immediately before oil is sprayed on it.　14.__

15. If an oil sprayer nozzle is rusty and gummy, it should be soaked in kerosene for a few days.　15.__

16. Chest x-ray examinations are required for school employees to check on their heart condition.　16.__

17. Auditoriums and assembly rooms usually require brighter lighting than gymnasiums.　17.

18. The national flag should be displayed on every school day, but not on legal holidays.　18.__

19. The soda-acid fire extinguisher is not affected by freezing temperatures.　19.__

20. Clear cold water should be used to rinse rubber tile floors after they have been mopped.   20.____

21. New asphalt tile floors require the use of a sealer or lacquer to seal the pores.   21.____

22. Soapsuds are often used to locate gas leaks in gas lines.   22.____

23. A kilowatt equals 1000 watts.   23.____

24. The very first step a custodian should take when a water pipe bursts is to call for a plumber.   24.____

25. *Rock Island Sheepswool* is a term usually applied to natural sponges.   25.____

26. There is less danger of electric shock when electric wires are touched with wet hands than with dry hands.   26.____

27. Air for ventilation of school buildings should never be recirculated.   27.____

28. Sweeping compound for use on linoleum and asphalt tile should contain sawdust, floor oil, and water wax.   28.____

29. Chlordane is useful as an insecticide for the control of crawling insects such as roaches.   29.____

30. Soda-acid fire extinguishers for use in school buildings usually have a gallon capacity.   30.____

31. Kick plates of doors should be lubricated about once a month.   31.____

32. A stillson wrench is usually used on heads and nuts of bolts.   32.____

33. No. 000 steel wool is coarser than No. 0 steel wool.   33.____

34. The preferred type of paint for the walls of school classrooms is a durable glossy enamel.   34.____

35. More accidents result from unsafe actions than from unsafe conditions.   35.____

36. The steam gauge cock should always be open when the boiler is operating.   36.____

37. When a wire carrying current becomes hot, it indicates that the fuse in the line has blown.   37.____

38. If the fusible plug of a boiler is coated with scale, it will melt at a lower temperature.   38.____

39. A water pump is usually primed with oil or grease.   39.____

40. Sharp-edged hand tools should usually be carried with the sharp edge down.   40.____

41. Using chisels with mushroomed heads is a safe practice if the user wears safety goggles.   41.____

42. The fire in a boiler furnace should be cleaned before banking it for the night.   42.____

43. School classrooms usually require weekly scrubbing in order to keep them acceptably clean.   43.____

44. Trisodium phosphate is a poor cleaning agent for oily or greasy surfaces.   44.____

45. Weathering of coal is a source of fuel waste.   45._

46. Standpipes usually supply water to the toilets and fountains on the upper floors of a   46._
building.

47. Goods subject to damage by heat should be stored near the ceiling of a storeroom if pos-   47._
sible.

48. Two light coats of wax on a floor are better than one good heavy coat.   48._

49. If a custodian sees a child defacing a corridor wall, he should not stop the child but   49._
should report him to the principal or teacher.

50. A carbon tetrachloride fire extinguisher can be effectively used to put out a fire in an elec- 50._
tric motor.

KEY (CORRECT ANSWERS)

1.	T	11.	F	21.	F	31.	F	41.	F
2.	F	12.	T	22.	T	32.	F	42.	T
3.	F	13.	F	23.	T	33.	F	43.	F
4.	T	14.	F	24.	F	34.	F	44.	F
5.	F	15.	T	25.	T	35.	T	45.	T
6.	T	16.	F	26.	F	36.	T	46.	F
7.	F	17.	F	27.	F	37.	F	47.	F
8.	F	18.	F	28.	F	38.	F	48.	T
9.	T	19.	F	29.	T	39.	F	49.	F
10.	T	20.	T	30.	T	40.	T	50.	T

EXAMINATION SECTION
TEST 1

DIRECTIONS: Each question or incomplete statement is followed by several suggested answers or completions. Select the one that BEST answers the question or completes the statement. *PRINT THE LETTER OF THE CORRECT ANSWER IN THE SPACE AT THE RIGHT.*

1. The BEST course of action to take to settle a job-related dispute that has arisen among two of your employees is to

   A. bring them both together, listen to their arguments, and then make a decision
   B. tell the two employees individually to settle their dispute
   C. tell both employees to submit their dispute in writing to you and then make a decision
   D. listen to the argument of each one separately and then make a decision

   1._____

2. A custodian accidentally discovers a bottle of whiskey in a staff member's desk. The BEST procedure for the custodian to follow is to

   A. verbally reprimand him and prefer departmental charges
   B. inform him that whiskey is not allowed in school buildings
   C. call a meeting of all the employees and tell them what you found
   D. do nothing as you do not want to embarrass the person

   2._____

3. A new employee under your supervision constantly reports late for work. The one of the following actions you should take FIRST is to

   A. admonish him in front of the other employees
   B. prefer charges against him
   C. transfer him to another school
   D. warn him that he must be on time

   3._____

4. The one of the following procedures that is BEST to follow when it is necessary to reprimand a worker is to

   A. issue the same reprimand to all your men
   B. avoid him so he won't feel bad
   C. speak to him privately about the matter
   D. tell him what he has done wrong immediately to teach the other employees a lesson

   4._____

5. The LEAST important factor to consider when evaluating the work of an employee is

   A. his grade on his civil service test
   B. the quality of his work
   C. his resourcefulness
   D. his attendance record

   5._____

6. The one of the following supervisory actions that a custodian should use LEAST often is   6.__
   to

   A. make periodic reports to his superior about the work of his men
   B. bring employees up on "charges" whenever they do anything wrong
   C. listen to staff grievances
   D. advise an employee concerning a personal problem

7. The MAIN supervisory responsibility of a custodian is to   7._

   A. foster policies of the board and the parents' organizations
   B. do his job so well that the students and employees like him
   C. make assignments to his employees
   D. keep the building and grounds in good operating condition

8. One of your employees verbally protests to you about your evaluation of his work.   8._
   The BEST way to handle him is to

   A. advise him of your lengthy and qualified experience
   B. tell him that you do not care to talk about it
   C. explain to him how you arrived at your evaluation
   D. tell him that since all the other employees are satisfied, he should withdraw his
      complaint

9. A custodian will BEST keep the morale of his men high by   9._

   A. giving praise for well-done work
   B. assigning good workers the most work
   C. personally helping each man in all the details of the man's job
   D. allowing special privileges for good work

10. In training maintenance personnel under the supervision of a custodian, the one of the   10._
    following that should be given LEAST consideration by the custodian is

    A. how the training is to be given
    B. who is to be trained
    C. when the training will be given
    D. how the school principal wants them to be trained

11. The BEST attitude for a custodian to follow in his dealings with the public is to   11._

    A. offer aid and cooperation to the public wherever possible
    B. show authority so that the public knows the limits to which they may make requests
    C. ignore the public since the custodian has a specific job to do
    D. refer the public to higher authority for solution of all their problems

12. The students playing in the schoolyard consistently lose rubber balls that land on the   12._
    school roof. They request that you, the custodian, retrieve these balls
    Of the following, the BEST procedure for you to follow is .

    A. teach them a lesson and refuse to retrieve the balls
    B. retrieve the balls and throw them into the incinerator
    C. one day a week retrieve the balls and return them to the students
    D. retrieve the balls and give them to a local children's charity

13. The president of a charitable organization requests a permit to use the school building. 13.____
You, the custodian, note that this same organization used the school previously and did
not observe the "no smoking" rules.
The BEST procedure for you to follow is to

   A. deny the organization a permit since they did not obey the school regulations
   before
   B. issue the permit without any questions since a large group is difficult to control
   C. inform the president that if any of his members continue to disregard the "no smoking" rules, future permits will not be issued
   D. inform the president that if any of his members continue to disregard the "no smoking" rules, you will evict them from the school building

14. Due to some grievances, parents occupy your school on a weekend and refuse to leave. 14.____
As the school principal is out of town and unavailable, the BEST procedure for you, the
custodian on duty, is to

   A. tell your employees to vacate the school
   B. call the police department
   C. cooperate with the parents on the take-over
   D. lock all the people in the school

15. An organization requests a permit to use the school auditorium from the hours of 7 P.M. 15.____
to 10 P.M. on a Tuesday evening. The organization also requests that its members be
allowed to enter the school earlier than 7 P.M. and leave later than 10 P.M.
The BEST procedure for you, the custodian, to follow is to

   A. inform the organization leader that the organization may only use the school from
   the hours of 7 P.M. to 10 P.M.
   B. issue the permit without saying anything as you want to maintain good public relations
   C. refer the matter to the school principal as you do not want to get involved
   D. ask the organization leader the reasons for the request and, if the request is fair,
   issue the permit and let the organization do as it pleases

16. Dog owners in the neighborhood have been disregarding the *curb your dog* signs and 16.____
walking their dogs on your school lawn. You find that this interferes with the operation of
powered lawn mowing equipment.
Your BEST procedure to follow is to

   A. put up a higher fence
   B. chase the people and dogs away
   C. tell the owners you will call the police department
   D. explain the problem to the owners and ask them to curb their dogs

17. A cleaner reports to the custodian that a particular schoolroom is consistently messy and 17.____
dirty. The one who is equally at fault as the students for this dirty room is the

   A. students' parents
   B. regular classroom teacher
   C. student peer groups
   D. cleaner for reporting the matter

18. A parent walks into a custodian's office and starts to shout at him about a claimed injustice to her child. The PROPER procedure for the custodian to follow is to

    A. call the police department
    B. summon the security guards
    C. vacate the office
    D. escort the parent to a guidance counselor

18._

19. A newspaper reporter visiting a school should normally be referred to the

    A. school principal
    B. school custodian engineer
    C. assistant superintendent of schools
    D. borough supervisor of school custodians

19._

20. The parents of children in the neighborhood of your school complain to you that their children cannot use the school playground after school hours because the gates are closed. The BEST procedure for you to follow is

    A. tell the parents the gates will remain closed after school hours
    B. arrange for the children to use a play street
    C. tell the parents to meet with the board on this matter
    D. try to arrange for the school gates to be open to a later hour after school hours

20._

21. Assume that there is a regulation requiring the men to notify the custodian when they intend to be absent. One of your men stays out without notifying you.
    Of the following, the FIRST thing that you should do is to

    A. discuss the matter with your supervisor
    B. find out the reason for the man's failure to comply with this regulation
    C. threaten the man with disciplinary action
    D. find out what the other custodians are doing about similar situations

21._

22. The members of a crew are LEAST likely to object to strict rules as long as

    A. they know who made them
    B. the rules are applied only occasionally as a disciplinary measure
    C. the rules are applied equally to all the workers
    D. they are posted in a public place

22._

23. Your supervisor complains to you that he could not find you at your assigned location and that the crew under your supervision was idle while you were away.
    Of the following, it is MOST important for you to

    A. improve your supervisory practices
    B. warn the men to look busy whenever they see one of the bosses
    C. disregard such an unreasonable complaint
    D. make certain you are rarely away from your assigned location

23._

24. Assume that the crew you supervise considers some of their routine work unpleasant.   24.____
    The BEST way to get these unpleasant tasks done is to

    A. rotate them among all your men
    B. assign them to easygoing workers who never complain
    C. use them as a means of disciplining habitual latecomers
    D. do them yourself

25. Assume that when a custodian arrives at a job location, he finds that a loud argument is   25.____
    going on between two of his men.
    Of the following, the MOST advisable action for him to take first is to

    A. send one of the men to another job
    B. find out what caused the argument
    C. ask one of the other men to tell him the cause of the argument
    D. take the men with him to his supervisor

KEY (CORRECT ANSWERS)

1.	A		11.	A
2.	B		12.	C
3.	D		13.	C
4.	C		14.	B
5.	A		15.	A
6.	B		16.	D
7.	D		17.	B
8.	C		18.	D
9.	A		19.	A
10.	D		20.	D

21.	B
22.	C
23.	A
24.	A
25.	B

TEST 2

DIRECTIONS: Each question or incomplete statement is followed by several suggested answers or completions. Select the one that BEST answers the question or completes the statement. *PRINT THE LETTER OF THE CORRECT ANSWER IN THE SPACE AT THE RIGHT.*

1. Of the following, the BEST reason for a custodian NOT allowing his employees to accept tips from people is that

   A. all employees would not be given equal treatment
   B. employees would become dishonest
   C. people are entitled to service without tips
   D. people in projects can't afford tips

1.__

2. Your attitude as a custodian to complaints by your employees should be that

   A. all employees like to complain
   B. if you let the worker "give off some steam," the complaint will disappear
   C. you will listen to them and try to correct the condition
   D. you will try to show the worker where he is wrong

2.__

3. A requisition would be filled out by a custodian in order to

   A. get supplies from the stockroom
   B. return to the stockroom supplies you haven't used
   C. find out the supplies you have on hand
   D. show that supplies were used up faster than expected

3.__

4. Assume that you are a custodian and have to write a report on a new employee who will finish his probationary period next month.
   Which one of the following would be the BEST reason for recommending that he be dropped from the job? He

   A. was late several times during the past five months for a total of 50 minutes
   B. is a slow worker compared to the other men
   C. insists on eating his lunch alone instead of with the other men
   D. is in the habit of accepting drinks from outsiders during working hours although you have often told him it is forbidden

4.__

5. It is MOST important that a report from a custodian to his superior be

   A. typewritten
   B. free of any mistakes in spelling or English
   C. accurate and have all the necessary facts
   D. brief to save time of all concerned

5.__

6. Suppose that you are a custodian and one of your men asks why you did not recommend him for an above-average work performance rating.
   You should tell him

   A. that above-average work reports can be recommended only by higher authority
   B. why you did not give him an above-average work report
   C. that you will recommend an above-average v/ork performance rating next year if he does better work
   D. how he can appeal his rating and help him write his appeal

6.__

7. Suppose that you are a custodian and one of your men is absent from work one day. You   7._____
    don't have any extra men and some of the work usually done by the absent man has to
    be finished that day.
    It would be BEST for you to

    A. call your men together and let them decide which one is to do the work
    B. shorten the lunch period and have each man do some of the work
    C. ask one of your better men to *pitch in* by doing a little extra work today
    D. explain to the buildings superintendent why it will not be possible to finish this work
        today

8. One of your men complains about a job you gave him. He is angry about getting the   8._____
    assignment. You don't think that the man is right in getting so upset.
    You should

    A. discuss the problem with him and explain why you gave him the job
    B. refer the man to your supervisor because he refuses to obey orders
    C. show the man that the whole matter is unimportant and a waste of time
    D. tell the man to do the job first and complain later

9. Two of your men start an argument while at work. As a custodian, you should   9._____

    A. ignore them; it is normal for men working together to have arguments
    B. stop them right away and find out what started the argument
    C. let them argue it out as long as they continue working and don't talk too loud
    D. speak to one of the men privately and tell him he is interfering with the work

10. Suppose you are a new custodian and you are put in charge of a crew of men whom you   10._____
    do not know and who have been working together for a few months.
    For a smooth changeover to your leadership, it would be BEST for you to

    A. let them continue working at their present assignments while you get to know them
        better
    B. tell the men to call their old supervisor if they have any trouble while you are learn-
        ing the job
    C. ask the most experienced man to take charge of the crew for a short while until you
        are more familiar with the work
    D. ask each man whether he is satisfied with what he is doing or wants a change

11. One of your men makes a suggestion for improving the method of doing the work. You   11._____
    don't think the suggestion is workable.
    You should, as a custodian,

    A. forget the idea since it isn't workable
    B. tell the man to try out the idea and hold him responsible if it doesn't work out
    C. discuss with the man why you think the idea won't work and praise him for his inter-
        est in the job
    D. point out to the man that he is wasting your time bringing up an idea that is not
        practical

12. Suppose that you and your supervisor are making an inspection of one of the buildings 12.__
you are responsible for cleaning. Your superior notices that the elevator in the building
has not been cleaned. You know that a new employee who has been on the job for only
three months is assigned
to this building. You should

    A. tell your supervisor that you will have the elevator cleaned and see that it is kept
clean in the future
    B. explain to your supervisor the trouble you have in training new employees
    C. find the new man and ask him to explain to you and your superior why the elevator
is not clean
    D. tell your supervisor that the elevator was clean when you made your last inspection

13. Suppose that your men were asked to work overtime in order to repair a water main 13.__
break. When the work is finished, your superior thanks you for the excellent work that
was done.
For you, a custodian, to tell your men about this would be

    A. *bad,* because this was a private conversation between you and your superior
    B. *good,* because your men will see that you are well-liked by your superior
    C. *bad,* because your men will think that they will be asked to work whenever there is
an emergency
    D. *good,* because it will show the men their cooperation is appreciated

14. When you, as a custodian, discuss a grievance with an employee, you should 14.__

    A. not tell the employee what you think of his complaint until a later date
    B. avoid any arguments with the employee
    C. convince the employee that there is no basis for this grievance
    D. tell the employee his complaint is justified

15. At a quarter to five, one of your employees tells you that the incinerator in his building has 15.__
much refuse in it and he is willing to work overtime to burn it.
If you give him permission to do this, it would be

    A. *good,* because it will save time the next day for other important work
    B. *bad,* because this is not an emergency for which overtime could be approved
    C. *good,* because tenants would not complain that refuse piles up and causes odors
    D. *bad,* because the law does not allow burning after 5:00 P.M.

16. Because of absences, you are left short-handed. 16.__
Which one of the following operations should you lay over so that you can cover the
MOST important work on a minimum basis?

    A. Incineration of garbage
    B. Sweeping the lobby
    C. Sweeping and washing the elevators
    D. Washing corridor windows

17. Suppose that one of your men who is doing good .work asks for a transfer to another custodian.
It would be BEST for you to

    A. have a private talk with the man to find out why he wants a transfer
    B. tell the man that the other custodian will also expect him to do good work
    C. approve the transfer without question because a dissatisfied man will do a poor job
    D. ask the other men in your crew if they are dissatisfied with your supervision

17.____

18. One of your experienced workers and a new employee are arguing about the correct way to do a job on which they are working together.
As a custodian, you should

    A. listen to both men and then tell them that they must learn to settle their argument without interrupting your work
    B. side with the older worker because he is more experienced
    C. listen to both men and then tell them how the work is to be done
    D. take one of the men off the job

18.____

19. Suppose that the department is introducing a new procedure for cleaning the hallways of buildings.
As a custodian, the BEST way for you to acquaint your men with this new procedure and to get them to use it is to

    A. wait until it has been tried out in another building and, if it is successful, put it into use in your building
    B. give each man a printed copy of the new procedure and set a deadline date by which each man is to read it and know it
    C. get your men together and explain the new procedure to them and how it will affect their work
    D. teach it to your best man and when he is familiar with it, ask him to teach it to the other men one at a time

19.____

20. Suppose that, as a custodian, you have finished *breaking in* a new employee. A few days later, you see the new man doing the job the wrong way.
You should

    A. immediately show the man what he is doing wrong and how to do it correctly
    B. assign him to some other work
    C. let your superior know that the new man cannot follow instructions
    D. say nothing because you may make the new man nervous

20.____

21. Suppose that a new type waxing machine is to be used in your building.
Of the following, the BEST way for you to teach your men how to use this machine is to

    A. give a talk on how to operate the machine
    B. demonstrate the operation and then have each man operate the machine under your supervision
    C. have the manufacturer give a talk on how to operate the machine
    D. give each man a set of carefully written instructions on how to operate the machine

21.____

22. When a custodian has to teach a man a new job, it would be MOST helpful for him to find out   22.__

    A.   how long the man has been with the department and how long he plans to stay
    B.   the man's dependability and willingness
    C.   the man's past record of cooperation with other workers
    D.   what the man already knows that will help him in learning the new job

23. When a new custodian comes on the job, it is LEAST important for him to know   23.__

    A.   the location of the buildings in the unit
    B.   how long the foremen have been there
    C.   the names of the men who work there
    D.   where the tools and equipment are kept

24. When you assign work to your men, it is usually BEST to   24.__

    A.   give each man the same amount of work
    B.   give the jobs that take the longest time to the senior men
    C.   assign work to each man according to his ability
    D.   let each man pick his own assignment

25. As a custodian, you will MOST likely be respected by your men if you   25.__

    A.   keep your personnel records simple and clear
    B.   offer them advice in solving their family problems
    C.   leave it to them to decide how a job is to be done
    D.   are fair and honest with them

KEY (CORRECT ANSWERS)

1.	C	11.	C
2.	C	12.	A
3.	A	13.	D
4.	D	14.	B
5.	C	15.	D
6.	B	16.	D
7.	C	17.	A
8.	A	18.	C
9.	B	19.	C
10.	A	20.	A

21.	B
22.	D
23.	B
24.	C
25.	D

———

TEST 3

1. Good public relations can be damaged by a custodian who treats tenants, fellow workers, friends, relatives, and the public with

   A. courtesy
   C. contempt
   B. consideration
   D. respect

   1.__

2. An office worker complains to a custodian that one of the cleaners broke off a branch of a plant which she kept on her desk and that she can identify the cleaner.
   The BEST thing for the custodian to do is to

   A. convince her that the plant will grow another branch eventually
   B. make the cleaner apologize and pay for a new plant out of his own pocket
   C. sympathize with the office worker and assure her that he will speak to the cleaner about it
   D. tell her not to bother him about her personal property

   2.__

3. When a new employee reports to a custodian on his first day on the job, the custodian SHOULD

   A. extend a hearty welcome and make the new employee feel welcome
   B. have the man sit and wait for a while before seeing him so that the employee realizes how busy the custodian is
   C. warn him of stern disciplinary action if he is late or absent excessively
   D. tell him he probably will have difficulty doing the work so that he doesn't become overconfident

   3.__

4. The one of the following subjects of a fire prevention training program which is MOST readily applied on the job is the

   A. elimination of fire hazards
   B. use of portable fire extinguishers
   C. knowledge of types of fires
   D. method of reporting fires

   4.__

5. A custodian who is a good supervisor will NOT

   A. tell his men what their jobs are and why they are important
   B. show his men how their jobs are to be done in the right way
   C. require some of the men to do their jobs in the presence of the supervisor demonstrating that they understand the job
   D. leave his men alone because they will always do their jobs correctly once they have received their instructions

   5.__

6. When a custodian sees a worker doing his job incorrectly, he should

   A. tell the worker to be more careful
   B. suspend the worker until he learns to do the job correctly
   C. tell the worker specifically how the job should be done
   D. scold the man

   6.__

7. An employee who is a good worker but is often late for work   7.____

    A. is lazy and should be dismissed
    B. cannot tell time
    C. can have no excuse for being late more than once a month
    D. should be questioned by his supervisor to try to find out why he is late

8. When starting any disciplinary action, a custodian who is a good supervisor should   8.____

    A. show his annoyance by losing his temper
    B. be apologetic
    C. be sarcastic
    D. be firm and positive

9. The BEST way for a custodian to maintain good employee morale is to   9.____

    A. avoid praising any one employee
    B. always have an alibi for his own mistakes
    C. encourage cliques by giving them information before giving it to other workers
    D. give adequate credit and praise when due

10. The BEST way for a custodian to tell if the night cleaners have done their work well is to check   10.____

    A. on how much cleaning material has been used
    B. on how much waste paper was collected
    C. the building for cleanliness
    D. the floor mops to see if they are still wet

11. The one of the following which is the BEST reason for introducing a training program is that the   11.____

    A. quality of work is above standard
    B. employees are all experienced
    C. accident rate is too high
    D. complaints are negligible

12. The FIRST step in training an inexperienced individual in a particular job is to   12.____

    A. put him to work and watch for mistakes
    B. put him to work and tell him to call for help if he needs it
    C. put him at ease and then find out what he knows about the work
    D. tell him to watch the least experienced worker on the job because the training is still fresh in his mind

13. As used in job analysis, the term *job breakdown* means   13.____

    A. any equipment failure
    B. any failure on the part of the worker to complete the job
    C. dividing the job into a series of steps
    D. reducing the number of workers by 50 percent

14. In dealing with the public, a custodian should be   14.__

    A. indulgent   B. courteous
    C. disagreeable   D. unavailable

15. If a custodian sees a group of people in front of his building preparing to form a picket   15.__
    line, he should

    A. turn on a lawn sprinkler to spray the pickets
    B. order the pickets off the sidewalk in front of the building
    C. show the pickets he is sympathetic with their complaint against the city
    D. contact his supervisor immediately for instructions

16. When electric service in a public building is to be shut off from 10 A.M. Tuesday to 11:30   16.__
    the next morning because a new electric feeder cable is being installed, the custodian
    should

    A. prepare a memo to all office supervisors in the building, notifying them of the situa-
       tion, and deliver a copy to each office as soon as possible
    B. prepare a notice of the impending power stoppage and post it in the lobby early
       Tuesday morning
    C. tell the electrical contractor to notify the tenants when he is about to shut off the
       power
    D. discontinue elevator service at 10 A.M. on Tuesday as an indication to the tenants
       that the power supply is off

17. Time standards for cleaning are of value ONLY if   17.__

    A. a bonus is promised if the time standards are beaten
    B. the cleaners determine the methods and procedures to be used
    C. accompanied by a completely detailed description of the methods to be used
    D. a schematic diagram of the area is made available to the cleaners

18. Of the following, the one which is the LEAST important factor in deciding that additional   18.__
    training is necessary for the men you supervise is that

    A. the quality of work is below standard
    B. supplies are being wasted
    C. too much time is required to do specific jobs
    D. the absentee rate has declined

19. To promote proper safety practices in the operation of power tools and equipment, the   19.__
    custodian should emphasize in meetings with his staff that

    A. every accident can be prevented through proper safety regulations
    B. proper safety practices will probably make future safety meetings unnecessary
    C. when safety rules are followed, tools and equipment will work better
    D. safety rules are based on past experience with the best methods of preventing
       accidents

20. As a custodian, a GOOD practical method to use in determining whether an employee is doing his job properly is to   20._____

    A. assume that if he asks no questions, he knows the work
    B. question him directly on details of the job
    C. inspect and follow-up the work which is assigned to him
    D. ask other employees how this employee is making out

21. If an employee continually asks how he should do his work, the custodian should   21._____

    A. dismiss him immediately
    B. pretend he does not hear him unless he persists
    C. explain the work carefully but encourage him to use his own judgment
    D. tell him not to ask so many questions

22. As a custodian, you have instructed an employee to wet mop a certain area. To be sure that the employee understands the instructions you have given him, you should   22._____

    A. ask him to repeat the instructions to you
    B. check with him after he has done the job
    C. watch him while he is doing the job
    D. repeat the instructions to the employee

23. As a custodian, one of your men disagrees with your evaluation of his work. Of the following, the BEST way to handle this situation would be to   23._____

    A. explain that you are in a better position to evaluate his work than he is
    B. tell him that since the other men are satisfied with your evaluation, he should accept their opinions
    C. explain the basis of your evaluation and discuss it with him
    D. refuse to discuss his complaint in order to maintain discipline

24. Of the following, the one which is NOT a purpose of a cleaning job breakdown is to   24._____

    A. eliminate unnecessary steps
    B. determine the type of floor wax to use
    C. rearrange the sequence of operations to save time
    D. combine steps or actions where practicable

25. The BEST method of making cleaning assignments in a large building is by means of   25._____

    A. daily rotation   B. specific assignment
    C. individual choice   D. chronological order

KEY (CORRECT ANSWERS)

1.	C		11.	C
2.	C		12.	C
3.	A		13.	C
4.	A		14.	B
5.	D		15.	D
6.	C		16.	A
7.	D		17.	C
8.	D		18.	D
9.	D		19.	D
10.	C		20.	C

21.	C
22.	A
23.	C
24.	B
25.	B

———————

MECHANICAL APTITUDE
TOOLS AND THEIR USE

EXAMINATION SECTION
TEST 1

Questions 1-16.

DIRECTIONS: Questions 1 through 16 refer to the tools shown below. The numbers in the answers refer to the numbers beneath the tools.
NOTE: These tools are NOT shown to scale

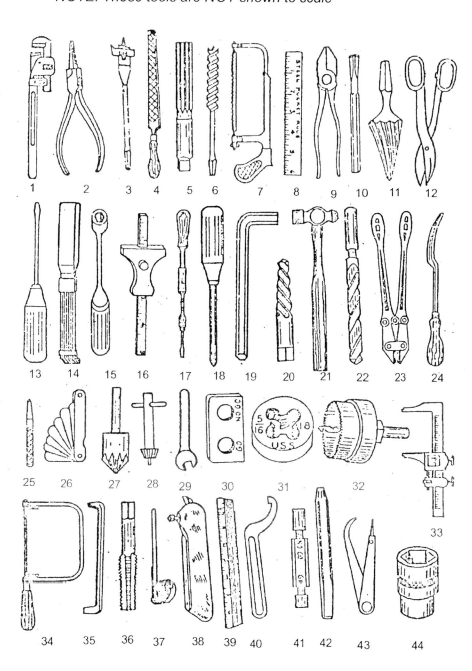

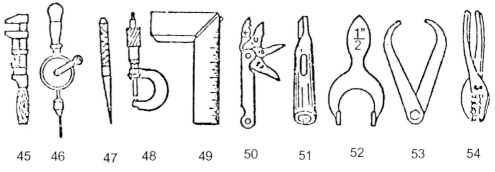

| 45 | 46 | 47 | 48 | 49 | 50 | 51 | 52 | 53 | 54 |

1. A 1" x 1" x 1/8" angle iron should be cut by using tool number

    A. 7   B. 12   C. 23   D. 42

2. To peen an iron rivet, you should use tool number

    A. 4   B. 7   C. 21   D. 43

3. The star "drill" is tool number

    A. 5   B. 10   C. 20   D. 22

4. To make holes in sheet metal for sheet metal screws, you should use tool number .

    A. 6   B. 10   C. 36   D. 46

5. To cut through a 3/8" diameter wire rope, you should use tool number

    A. 12   B. 23   C. 42   D. 54

6. To remove cutting burrs from the inside of a steel pipe, you should use tool number

    A. 5   B. 11   C. 14   D. 20

7. The depth of a bored hole may be measured MOST accurately with tool number

    A. 8   B. 16   C. 26   D. 41

8. If the marking on the blade of tool number 7 reads:12"-32", the 32 refers to the

    A. length   B. thickness   C. weight
    D. number of teeth per inch

9. If tool number 6 bears the mark "5", it should be used to drill holes having a diameter of

    A. 5/32"   B. 5/16"   C. 5/8"   D. 5"

10. To determine MOST quickly the number of threads per inch on a bolt, you should use tool number

    A. 8   B. 16   C. 26   D. 50

11. Wood screws, located in positions where the headroom does not permit the use of an ordinary screwdriver, may be removed by using tool number

    A. 17   B. 28   C. 35   D. 46

12. To remove a broken-off piece of 1/2" diameter pipe from a fitting, you should use tool number   12.____

    A. 5   B. 11   C. 20   D. 36

13. The outside diameter of a bushing may be measured MOST accurately with tool number   13.____

    A. 8   B. 26   C. 33   D. 43

14. To re-thread a stud hole in the casting of an elevator motor, you should use tool number   14.____

    A. 5   B. 20   C. 22   D. 36

15. To enlarge slightly a bored hole in a steel plate, you should use tool number   15.____

    A. 5   B. 11   C. 20   D. 36

16. The term "16 oz." should be applied to tool number   16.____

    A. 1   B. 12   C. 21   D. 42

KEYS (CORRECT ANSWERS)

1.	A	9.	B
2.	C	10.	D
3.	B	11.	C
4.	D	12.	C
5.	B	13.	C
6.	B	14.	D
7.	B	15.	A
8.	D	16.	C

TEST 2

Questions 1-11.

DIRECTIONS: Questions 1 through 11 refer to the instruments listed below. Each instrument is listed with an identifying number in front of it.

1 - Hygrometer	6 - Oscilloscope	11 - 6-foot folding rule
2 - Ammeter	7 - Frequency meter	12 - Architect's scale
3 - Voltmeter	8 - Micrometer	13 - Planimeter
4 - Wattmeter	9 - Vernier calliper	14 - Engineer's scale
5 - Megger	10 - Wire gage	15 - Ohmmeter

1. The instrument that should be used to *accurately* measure the resistance of a 4,700‾ohm resistor is number

    A. 3   B. 4   C. 7   D. 15

2. To measure the current in an electrical circuit, the instrument that should be used is number

    A. 2   B. 7   C. 8   D. 15

3. To measure the insulation resistance of a rubber-covered electrical cable, the instrument that should be used is number

    A. 4   B. 5   C. 8   D. 15

4. An AC motor is hooked up to a power distribution box. In order to check the voltage at the motor terminals, the instrument that should be used is number

    A. 2   B. 3   C. 4   D. 7

5. To measure the shaft diameter of a motor *accurately* to one-thousandth of an inch, the instrument that should be used is number

    A. 8   B. 10   C. 11   D. 14

6. The instrument that should be used to determine whether 25 Hz. or 60 Hz. is present in an electrical circuit is number

    A. 4   B. 5   C. 7   D. 8

7. Of the following, the *proper* instrument to use to determine the diameter of the conductor of a piece of electrical hookup wire is number

    A. 10   B. 11   C. 12   D. 14

8. The amount of electrical power being used in a balanced three-phase circuit should be measured with number

    A. 2   B. 3   C. 4   D. 5

9. The electrical wave form at a given point in an electronic circuit can be observed with number

    A. 2   B. 3   C. 6   D. 7

10. The *proper* instrument to use for measuring the width of a door is number   10.____

    A. 11   B. 12   C. 13   D. 14

11. A one-inch hole with a tolerance of plus or minus three-thousandths is reamed in a steel   11.____
block. The *proper* instrument to accurately check the diameter of the hole is number

    A. 8   B. 9   C. 11   D. 14

12. An oilstone is LEAST likely to be used correctly to sharpen a   12.____

    A. scraper   B. chisel   C. knife   D. saw

13. To cut the ends of a number of lengths of wood at an angle of 45 degrees, it would be   13.____
BEST to use a

    A. mitre-box   B. protractor   C. triangle   D. wooden rule

14. A gouge is a tool used for   14.____

    A. planing wood smooth   B. grinding metal
    C. drilling steel   D. chiseling wood

15. Holes are usually countersunk when installing   15.____

    A. carriage bolts   B. lag screws
    C. flat-head screws   D. square nuts

16. A tool that is *generally* used to slightly elongate a round hole in scrap-iron is a   16.____

    A. rat-tail file   B. reamer   C. drill   D. rasp

17. When the term "10-24" is used to specify a machine screw, the number 24 refers to the   17.____

    A. number of screws per pound   B. diameter of the screw
    C. length of the screw   D. number of threads per inch

18. If you were unable to tighten a nut by means of a ratchet wrench because, although the   18.____
nut turned on with the forward movement of the wrench, it turned off with the backward
movement, you should

    A. make the nut hand-tight before using the wrench
    B. reverse the ratchet action
    C. put a few drops of oil on the wrench
    D. use a different socket in the handle

19. If you were installing a long wood screw and found you were unable to drive this screw   19.____
more than three-quarters of its length by the use of a properly-fitting straight-handled
screwdriver, the *proper* SUBSEQUENT action would be for you to

    A. take out the screw and put soap on it
    B. change to the use of a screwdriver-bit and brace
    C. take out the screw and drill a shorter hole before redriving
    D. use a pair of pliers on the blade of the screwdriver

20. Good practice requres that the end of a pipe to be installed in a plumbing system be reamed to remove the inside burr after it has been cut to length. The *purpose* of this reaming is to

   A. restore the original inside diameter of the pipe at the end
   B. remove loose rust
   C. make the threading of the pipe easier
   D. finish the pipe accurately to length

20

KEYS (CORRECT ANSWERS)

1.	D		11.	B
2.	A		12.	D
3.	B		13.	A
4.	B		14.	D
5.	A		15.	C
6.	C		16.	A
7.	A		17.	D
8.	C		18.	A
9.	C		19.	A
10.	A		20.	A

ARITHMETICAL REASONING
EXAMINATION SECTION
TEST 1

DIRECTIONS: Each question or incomplete statement is followed by several suggested answers or completions. Select the one that BEST answers the question or completes the statement. *PRINT THE LETTER OF THE CORRECT ANSWER IN THE SPACE AT THE RIGHT.*

1. A custodial assistant takes an average of forty minutes to mop 1,000 square feet of floor.
   The amount of time this custodial assistant should take to mop the floor of a rectangular corridor eight feet wide by sixty feet long is, on the average, MOST NEARLY _____ minutes.
   A. 10   B. 20   C. 30   D. 40   1.___

2. An auditorium eighty feet by 100 feet must be swept in one hour.
   If each custodial assistant takes fifteen minutes to sweep 1,000 square feet of auditorium area, the number of custodial assistants that must be assigned to complete the sweeping in one hour is
   A. 1   B. 2   C. 3   D. 4   2.___

3. A detergent manufacturer recommends mixing 8 ounces of detergent in one gallon of water to prepare a cleaning solution.
   The amount of the same detergent which should be mixed with thirty gallons of water to obtain the same strength cleaning solution is _____ ounces.
   A. 24   B. 30   C. 240   D. 380   3.___

4. The floor area of a corridor 8 feet wide and 72 feet long is MOST NEARLY _____ square feet.
   A. 80   B. 420   C. 580   D. 870   4.___

5. A water tank that is 5 feet in diameter and 30 feet high has a volume of MOST NEARLY _____ cubic feet.
   A. 150   B. 250   C. 600   D. 1,200   5.___

6. The circumference of a circle with a radius of 5 inches is MOST NEARLY _____ inches.
   A. 31.3   B. 30.0   C. 20.1   D. 13.4   6.___

7. Suppose that you are the custodian-engineer and an employee works for you at the rate of $8.70 per hour with time and one-half paid for time worked after 40 hours in one week. His gross pay for working 53 hours in one week is MOST NEARLY
   A. $461.10   B. $482.10   C. $487.65   D. $517.65   7.___

8. Suppose that you are the custodian-engineer and one of
   your employees has gotten gross earnings of $437.10 for
   the week, all of which is subject to deductions at the
   rate of 4.8%.
   The amount which should be deducted from the employee's
   gross earnings for the week is MOST NEARLY
       A. $2.10   B. $14.70   C. $17.70   D. $20.97

    8.___

9. The directions on the label of a bottle of detergent
   call for mixing four ounces of detergent with one gallon
   of water to make a cleaning solution for washing floors.
   In order to obtain a larger amount of solution of the
   same strength, one quart of the detergent should be
   mixed with _____ gallons of water.
       A. 2   B. 4   C. 6   D. 8

    9.___

10. The area of a lawn which is 58 feet wide by 96 feet long
    is MOST NEARLY _____ square feet.
        A. 5,000   B. 5,500   C. 6,000   D. 6,500

    10.___

11. In a building which is heated by an oil-fired boiler,
    2,100 gallons of fuel oil were burned in a period in
    which the degree days reached a total of 1,400.
    If all other conditions remained constant, the number
    of gallons of fuel oil that would be burned in this
    building during a period in which the degree days reached
    a total of 3,600 is
        A. 2,400   B. 2,900   C. 4,800   D. 5,400

    11.___

12. The instructions for mixing a powdered cleaner in water
    state, *Mix three ounces of powder in a 14-quart pail
    three-quarters full of water.* A cleaner asks you how
    much powdered cleaner he should use in a mop truck con-
    taining 28 gallons of water to obtain the same strength
    solution.
    The CORRECT answer is _____ ounces of powder.
        A. 6   B. 8   C. 24   D. 32

    12.___

13. A custodian-engineer wishes to order sponges in the most
    economical manner.
    Keeping in mind that large sponges can be cut up into
    many smaller sizes, the one of the following that has
    the LEAST cost per cubic inch of sponge is
        A. 2" x 4" x 6" sponges @ $.48
        B. 4" x 8" x 12" sponges @ $2.88
        C. 4" x 6" x 36" sponges @ $9.60
        D. 6" x 8" x 32" sponges @ $19.20

    13.___

14. Two cleaners swept four corridors in 24 minutes. Each
    corridor measured 12 feet x 176 feet.
    The space swept per man per minute was MOST NEARLY _____
    square feet.
        A. 50   B. 90   C. 180   D. 350

    14.___

15. Kerosene costs 60 cents a quart.   15.___
At that rate, two gallons would cost
    A. $2.40   B. $3.60   C. $4.80   D. $6.00

16. The instructions on a container of cleaning compound   16.___
states, *Mix one pound of compound in 5 gallons of water.*
Using these instructions, the amount of compound which
should be added to 15 quarts of water is MOST likely
_____ ounces.
    A. 3   B. 8   C. 12   D. 48

17. Suppose that you are the custodian-engineer and one of   17.___
your employees has gross earnings of $582.80 for the
week, all of which is subject to Social Security deductions at the rate of 4.8%.
The amount which should be deducted from the employee's
gross earnings for the week is MOST NEARLY
    A. $2.80   B. $19.60   C. $23.60   D. $27.96

18. Suppose that you are a custodian-engineer and an employee   18.___
works for you at the rate of $11.60 per hour with time
and one-half paid for time worked after 40 hours in one
week.
His gross pay for working 53 hours in one week is MOST
NEARLY
    A. $614.80   B. $642.80   C. $650.20   D. $690.20

19. The volume, in cubic feet, of a cylindrical tank 6 feet   19.___
in diameter x 35 feet long is MOST NEARLY
    A. 210   B. 990   C. 1,260   D. 3,960

20. A room 12 feet wide by 25 feet long has a floor area of   20.___
_____ square feet.
    A. 37   B. 200   C. 300   D. 400

21. How many hours will it take a worker to sweep a floor   21.___
space of 2,800 square feet if he sweeps at the rate of
800 square feet per hour?
    A. 8   B. $6\frac{1}{2}$ C. $3\frac{1}{2}$ D. $2\frac{1}{2}$

22. One gallon of water contains   22.___
    A. 2 quarts   B. 4 quarts   C. 2 pints   D. 4 pints

23. A standard cleaning solution is prepared by mixing 4   23.___
ounces of detergent powder in 2 gallons of water.
The number of ounces of detergent powder needed for the
same strength solution in 5 gallons of water is
    A. 4   B. 6   C. 8   D. 10

24. The ceiling of a room which measures 20 feet x 30 feet   24.___
is to be given two coats of paint.
If one gallon of paint will cover 500 square feet, the
two coats of paint will require a MINIMUM of ____ gallons.
    A. 1.5   B. 2   C. 2.4   D. 3.2

25. The floor area of a room which measures 10 feet long by   25.___
    10 feet wide is _____ square feet.
         A. 20   B. 40   C. 100   D. 1,000

_____

KEY (CORRECT ANSWERS)

1. B		11. D
2. B		12. D
3. C		13. B
4. C		14. C
5. C		15. C
6. A		16. C
7. D		17. D
8. D		18. D
9. D		19. B
10. B		20. C

21. C
22. B
23. D
24. C
25. C

_____

SOLUTIONS TO PROBLEMS

1. $(8')(60') = 480$ sq.ft. Let x = required time in minutes.
    Then, $\frac{40}{1000} = \frac{x}{480}$. Solving, x = 19.2 or nearly 20.

2. $(80')(100') = 8000$ sq.ft. Each custodian can sweep $(1000)(4)$
    $= 4000$ sq.ft. in 1 hour. Then, $8000 \div 4000 = 2$.

3. $(8)(30) = 240$ ounces

4. $(8')(72') = 576$ sq.ft. or nearly 580 sq.ft.

5. Volume $= (\pi)(2.5')^2(30') \approx 589$ cu.ft. or nearly 600 cu.ft.

6. Circumference $= (2\pi)(5") \approx 31.3$ sq.in.

7. $(\$8.70)(40) + (\$13.05)(13) = \$517.65$

8. $(\$437.10)(.048) \approx \$20.97$

9. 1 quart = 32 oz. Then, $32 \div 4 = 8$ gallons of water

10. $(58')(96') = 5568$ sq.ft., which is closest to 5500 sq.ft.

11. Let x = number of gallons. Then, $\frac{2100}{1400} = \frac{x}{3600}$. Solving, x = 5400

12. $(.75)(14)(.25) = 2.625$ gallons of water. Let x = number of
    ounces of powder needed. Then, $\frac{3}{2.625} = \frac{x}{28}$. Solving, x = 32

13. For selection B, $(4")(8")(12") = 384$ cu.in., and the cost per
    cubic inch = $\$2.88 \div 384 = \$.0075$. This is lower than
    selections A ($\$.01$), C ($\$.011$), or D ($\$.015$).

14. Two men sweep $(4)(12')(176') = 8448$ total sq.ft. in 24 min. =
    352 sq.ft. per min. Each man sweeps 176 sq.ft. per min $\approx$
    180 sq.ft. per min.

15. Two gallons = 8 quarts. Then, $(\$.60)(8) = \$4.80$

16. 15 quarts = 3.75 gallons of water. Let x = required number of
    ounces of compound. Then, $\frac{16}{5} = \frac{x}{3.75}$. Solving, x = 12

17. $(\$582.80)(.048) \approx \$27.96$

18. $(\$11.60)(40) + (\$17.40)(13) = \$690.20$

19. Volume = $(\pi)(3')^2(35') \approx 990$ cu.ft.

20. $(12')(25') = 300$ sq.ft.

21. $2800 \div 800 = 3\frac{1}{2}$ hours

22. One gallon = 4 quarts

23. Let x = required number of ounces. Then, $\frac{4}{2} = \frac{x}{5}$. Solving, x = 1

24. 2 coats means $(2)(20')(30') = 1200$ sq.ft. Then, $1200 \div 500 = 2.4$ gallons

25. $(10')(10') = 100$ sq.ft.

TEST 2

DIRECTIONS: Each question or incomplete statement is followed by several suggested answers or completions. Select the one that BEST answers the question or completes the statement. *PRINT THE LETTER OF THE CORRECT ANSWER IN THE SPACE AT THE RIGHT.*

1. Assume that a certain elevator starter is at work 8 hours a day, which includes 1 hour for lunch and two 15-minute relief periods. The rest of the workday the starter is performing his duties.
   If the starter works 4 days, the TOTAL amount of time the starter will actually be performing his duties is _____ hours.
   A. 24   B. 26   C. 28   D. 32   1.___

2. Assume that a certain bank of 18 elevators operating at full capacity could move 3,240 passengers an hour from the main lobby.
   The number of passengers that one of these elevators could move from the lobby every 15 minutes is, on the average,
   A. 12   B. 22   C. 45   D. 180   2.___

3. In a certain agency, the amount of absence due to injury or illness was an average of 6 hours a month for each employee.
   If this agency had 335 employees, the TOTAL number of hours lost in a year due to injury or sickness was
   A. 4,020   B. 20,100   C. 24,120   D. 28,140   3.___

4. Assume that in a certain building the elevators must handle 16% of the building population during a peak traffic period.
   If the building population is 2,825, the TOTAL number of people the elevators must handle during a peak traffic period is
   A. 396   B. 424   C. 436   D. 452   4.___

5. From his coin bank, a boy took 3 half dollars, 8 quarters, 7 dimes, 6 nickels, and 9 pennies to deposit in his school savings account.
   Express in dollars and cents the TOTAL amount of money he deposited.
   A. $2.82   B. $4.59   C. $6.42   D. $7.52   5.___

6. If a roast that requires 1 hour and 40 minutes of roasting time has been in the oven for 55 minutes, how many more minutes of roasting time are required?
   A. 30   B. 36   C. 45   D. 55   6.___

7. On the first day of its drive, a school raised $40, which   7.__
   was 33 1/3% of its Red Cross quota.
   How much was the quota?
      A. $120   B. $130   C. $140   D. $150

8. When 0.750 is divided by 0.875, the answer is MOST NEARLY   8.__
      A. 0.250   B. 0.312   C. 0.624   D. 0.857

9. The circumference of a 6-inch diameter circle is MOST   9.__
   NEARLY ____ feet.
      A. 1.57   B. 2.1   C. 2.31   D. 4.24

10. An 18" piece of cable that weighs 3 pounds per foot has a   10.__
    total weight of ____ pounds.
       A. 5.5   B. 4.5   C. 3.0   D. 1.5

11. The sum of 0.135, 0.040, 0.812, and 0.961 is   11.__
       A. 1.424   B. 1.625   C. 1.843   D. 1.948

12. If an elevator carries a load of 1,600 pounds uniformly   12.__
    distributed on a 4 feet by 5 feet floor, the weight per
    square foot is ____ pounds.
       A. 98   B. 80   C. 65   D. 40

13. If one cubic inch of lead weighs one-quarter of a pound,   13.__
    the weight of a bar of lead 1" high by 2" wide by 8" long
    is ____ pounds.
       A. 1.8   B. 2.5   C. 3.1   D. 4

14. Assume that 8 mechanics have been assigned to do a job   14.__
    that must be finished in 5 days. At the end of 3 days,
    the men have completed only half the job.
    In order to complete the job on time in the remaining
    2 days, the MINIMUM number of extra men that should be
    assigned is
       A. 2   B. 3   C. 4   D. 6

15. An elevator supply manufacturer quotes a list price of   15.__
    $625 less 10 and 5 percent for ten contactors.
    The actual cost for these ten contactors is MOST NEARLY
       A. $562   B. $554   C. $534   D. $522

16. To find the largest number of passengers, including the   16.__
    operator, allowed to ride in an elevator, divide the
    rated capacity of the elevator by 150.
    According to this rule, what is the LARGEST number of
    passengers NOT counting the operator that may be carried
    in an elevator with a rated capacity of 3,000 lbs.?
       A. 18   B. 19   C. 20   D. 21

17. Suppose that the work schedule for operators is 5 days a   17.__
    week, 8 hours a day.
    In a period of 4 weeks, with no holidays, how many hours
    will you be required to be on duty?
       A. 160   B. 180   C. 200   D. 225

18. Mr. Jones takes $100 to cover his expenses for a week.   18.___
He spends $3.00 for carfare coming to work and $3.00 for
carfare going home. He buys a 50¢ newspaper each day
and spends $8.00 for lunch·and $2.50 for cigarettes
each day.
How much money does he have left at the end of a 5-day
work week?
   A. $15.00   B. $27.50   C. $50.00   D. $85.00

19. Twelve hundred employees work in an office building.   19.___
Twenty percent of these employees work on the 4th floor
and 25% work on the 5th floor.
The TOTAL number of employees who work on the 4th and
5th floors together is
   A. 240   B. 300   C. 540   D. 660

20. An elevator makes one roundtrip every 5 minutes, on the   20.___
average.
How many roundtrips does it make between 8:15 A.M. and
9:45 A.M.?
   A. 12   B. 18   C. 20   D. 22

21. The floor of an elevator car measures 7 feet by 8 feet   21.___
6 inches.
How many square feet of linoleum would be needed to
cover this floor?
   A. 31   B. 42   C. $59\frac{1}{2}$ D. $62\frac{1}{2}$

Questions 22-25.

DIRECTIONS: Each question consists of a statement. You are to
indicate whether the statement is TRUE (T) or FALSE (F).

22. In a city building, there are 20 elevators. If on one   22.___
day five percent of the elevators are out of order, the
number of elevators out of order is 2.

23. An elevator operator puts in 32 hours of overtime in   23.___
January, 26 hours in February, 10 hours in March, 10
hours in April, and 27 hours in May. The average amount
of overtime this operator worked per month for these five
months is 21 hours.

24. A large city building normally has 45 elevator operators   24.___
on its day shift. The vacation rules require that only
1/5 be allowed away at any time. The number of operators
that may be on vacation at one time is nine.

25. In a six-story city building, there are 13 offices on the   25.___
first floor, 19 offices on the second floor, 18 offices
on the third floor, 17 offices on the fourth floor, 21
offices on the fifth floor, and 23 offices on the sixth
floor. The total number of offices in this building is
109.

KEY (CORRECT ANSWERS)

1.	B	11.	D
2.	C	12.	B
3.	C	13.	D
4.	D	14.	C
5.	B	15.	C
6.	C	16.	B
7.	A	17.	A
8.	D	18.	A
9.	A	19.	C
10.	B	20.	B

21. C
22. F
23. T
24. T
25. F

SOLUTIONS TO PROBLEMS

1. 4(8-1-.5) = 26 hours

2. Each elevator can move 3240 ÷ 18 = 180 passengers per hour, which = 45 passengers per 15 minutes.

3. (335)(6)(12) = 24,120 hours per year.

4. (2825)(.16) = 452

5. (3)(.50) + (8)(.25) + (7)(.10) + (6)(.05) + (9)(.01) = $4.59

6. 1 hr. 40 min. - 55 min. = 100 min. - 55 min. = 45 min.

7. $40 ÷ $33\frac{1}{3}$% = $40 ÷ $\frac{1}{3}$ = $120

8. .750 ÷ .875 ≈ .857

9. Circumference = $(\frac{1}{2}')(\pi)$ ≈ 1.57'

10. 18" ÷ 12" = 1.5. Then, (1.5)(3) = 4.5 lbs.

11. .135 + .040 + .812 + .961 = 1.948

12. (4')(5') = 20 sq.ft. Then, 1600 ÷ 20 = 80 lbs. per sq.ft.

13. (1")(2")(8") = 16 cu.in. Then, $(16)(\frac{1}{4})$ = 4 pounds

14. 8 men × 3 cars = 50% of work; 24 man-days = 50% of work; 48 man-days = 100%; 24 man-days ÷ 2 days = 12 men per day = 4 extra men

15. ($625)(.90)(.95) ≈ $534

16. 3000 ÷ 150 = 20 people, including the operator. Thus, only 19 passengers are allowed.

17. (8)(5)(4) = 160 hours

18. $100 - 5($3.00+$3.00+$.50+$8.00+$2.50) = $15.00

19. (1200)(20%+25%) = (1200)(.45) = 540

20. 9:45 AM - 8:15 AM = 90 min. Then, 90 ÷ 5 = 18 roundtrips

21. $(7')(8\frac{1}{2}')$ = $59\frac{1}{2}$ sq.ft.

22. False; (20)(.05) = 1, not 2.

23. True. $(32+26+10+10+27) \div 5 = 21$

24. True. $(45)(\frac{1}{5}) = 9$

25. False. $13 + 19 + 18 + 17 + 21 + 23 = 111$, not 109

TEST 3

DIRECTIONS: Each question or incomplete statement is followed by several suggested answers or completions. Select the one that BEST answers the question or completes the statement. *PRINT THE LETTER OF THE CORRECT ANSWER IN THE SPACE AT THE RIGHT.*

1. When 60,987 is added to 27,835, the answer is   1.___
   A. 80,712   B. 80,822   C. 87,712   D. 88,822

2. The sum of 693 + 787 + 946 + 355 + 731 is   2.___
   A. 3,512   B. 3,502   C. 3,412   D. 3,402

3. When 2,586 is subtracted from 3,003, the answer is   3.___
   A. 417   B. 527   C. 1,417   D. 1,527

4. When 1.32 is subtracted from 52.6, the answer is   4.___
   A. 3.94   B. 5.128   C. 39.4   D. 51.28

5. When 56 is multiplied by 438, the answer is   5.___
   A. 840   B. 4,818   C. 24,528   D. 48,180

6. When 8.7 is multiplied by .34, the answer is MOST NEARLY   6.___
   A. 2.9   B. 3.0   C. 29.5   D. 29.6

7. When ½ is divided by 2/3, the answer is   7.___
   A. 1/3   B. 3/4   C. 1 1/3   D. 3

8. When 8,340 is divided by 38, the answer is MOST NEARLY   8.___
   A. 210   B. 218   C. 219   D. 220

9. Assume that a helper earns $5.58 an hour and that he   9.___
   works 250 seven-hour days a year.
   His gross yearly salary will be
   A. $9,715   B. $9,765   C. $9,825   D. $9,890

10. On a certain map, a distance of 10 miles is represented   10.___
    by ½ inch.
    If two towns are 3½ inches apart on this map, express,
    in miles, the actual distance between the two towns.
    A. 70   B. 80   C. 90   D. 100

11. The area of the triangle shown at the   11.___
    right is _____ square inches.
    A. 120
    B. 240
    C. 360
    D. 480

12. The sum of 1/3 + 2/5 + 5/6 is   12.___
    A. 1 17/30   B. 1 3/5   C. 1 5/8   D. 1 5/6

13. The sum of the following dimensions, 3'2¼", 0'8 7/8",   13.___
    2'6 3/8", 2'9 3/4", and 1'0", is
    A. 9'2 7/8"   B. 10'3¼"
    C. 10'7 3/7"   D. 11'4¼"

14. If the scale of a drawing is 1/8" to the foot, then a   14.___
    ½" measurement on the drawing would represent an actual
    length of _____ feet.
    A. 2   B. 4   C. 8   D. 16

15. Assume that an area measures 78 feet by 96 feet.   15.___
    The number of square feet in this area is
    A. 7,478   B. 7,488   C. 7,498   D. 7,508

16. If a can of paint costs $17.50, four dozen cans of this   16.___
    paint will cost
    A. $837.50   B. $840.00   C. $842.50   D. $845.00

17. The number of square feet in 1 square yard is   17.___
    A. 3   B. 6   C. 9   D. 12

18. The sum of 4½ inches, 3¼ inches, and 7½ inches is 1 foot   18.___
    _____ inches.
    A. 3   B. 3¼   C. 3½   D. 4

19. If a room is 10 feet by 18 feet, the number of square   19.___
    feet of floor space in it is
    A. 1,800   B. 180   C. 90   D. 28

20. A jacket that was marked at $12.50 was sold for $10.   20.___
    What was the rate of discount on the marked price?
    A. 10%   B. 15%   C. 18%   D. 20%

Questions 21-25.

DIRECTIONS: Each question consists of a statement. You are to
               indicate whether the statement is TRUE (T) or FALSE (F).

21. Three-eighths (3/8") of an inch is equivalent to .0375".   21.___

22. A floor measuring 12 feet by 9 feet contains 36 sq.ft.   22.___

23. A box measuring 18 inches square and 16 inches deep will   23.___
    have a volume of 36 cubic feet.

24. If the charge for a long distance telephone call is 50¢   24.___
    for the first 5 minutes and 7¢ for each minute after that,
    then for 85¢ a person could speak for 10 minutes.

25. If 15 gallons of gasoline cost $14.85 and you use up
    10 gallons, then the value of the gasoline which is
    still left is $4.95.

25.___

_____

KEY (CORRECT ANSWERS)

1. D		11. A	
2. A		12. A	
3. A		13. B	
4. D		14. B	
5. C		15. B	
6. B		16. B	
7. B		17. C	
8. C		18. B	
9. B		19. B	
10. A		20. D	

21. F
22. F
23. F
24. T
25. T

_____

SOLUTIONS TO PROBLEMS

1. $60,987 + 27,835 = 88,822$

2. $693 + 787 + 946 + 355 + 731 = 3512$

3. $3003 - 2586 = 417$

4. $52.6 - 1.32 = 51.28$

5. $(56)(438) = 24,528$

6. $(8.7)(.34) = 2.958 \approx 3.0$

7. $\dfrac{1}{2} \div \dfrac{2}{3} = \dfrac{1}{2} \cdot \dfrac{3}{2} = \dfrac{3}{4}$

8. $8340 \div 38 \approx 219.47 \approx 219$

9. $(\$5.58)(7)(250) = \$9765$

10. $3\frac{1}{2}'' \div \frac{1}{2}'' = 7$. Then, $(7)(10) = 70$ miles

11. Area $= (\frac{1}{2})(10'')(24'') = 120$ sq.in.

12. $\dfrac{1}{3} + \dfrac{2}{5} + \dfrac{5}{6} = \dfrac{10}{30} + \dfrac{12}{30} + \dfrac{25}{30} = \dfrac{47}{30} = 1\dfrac{17}{30}$

13. $3'2\frac{1}{4}'' + 0'8\frac{7}{8}'' + 2'6\frac{3}{8}'' + 2'9\frac{3}{4}'' + 1'0'' = 8'25\frac{18}{8}'' = 10'3\frac{1}{4}''$

14. $\frac{1}{2}'' \div \frac{1}{8}'' = 4$. Then, $(4)(1 \text{ ft.}) = 4$ ft.

15. $(78')(96') = 7488$ sq.ft.

16. $(48)(\$17.50) = \$840.00$

17. 1 sq.yd. $= (3)(3) = 9$ sq.ft.

18. $4\frac{1}{2}'' + 3\frac{1}{4}'' + 7\frac{1}{2}'' = 14\frac{5}{4}'' = 1$ foot $3\frac{1}{4}$ inches

19. $(10')(18') = 180$ sq.ft.

20. $\$12.50 - \$10 = \$2.50$. Then, $\$2.50 \div \$12.50 = .20 = 20\%$

21. False. $\frac{3}{8}'' = .375''$, not $.0375''$

22. False. (12')(9') = 108 sq.ft., not 36 sq.ft.

23. False. (18")(18")(16") = 5184 cu.in. = 3 cu.ft., not 36 cu.ft.
    Note: 1 cu.ft. = 1728 cu.in.

24. True. The cost for 10 minutes = .50 + (.07)(10-5) = .85

25. True. $14.85 ÷ 15 = $.99 per gallon. The value of 5 gallons
    = (5)($.99) = $4.95

THE USE AND CARE OF TOOLS

CONTENTS

d. Scrapers
e. Punches
f. Awls
g. Shears, Nippers, and Pincers h. Bolt, Cable, and Glass Cutters
i. Pipe and Tube Cutters, and Flaring Tools
j. Reamers
k. Taps and Dies
l. Thread Chasers
m. Screw and Tap Extractors

THE USE AND CARE OF TOOLS

I. INTRODUCTION

1. Definitions

    a. Handtools are defined as hand powered and hand operated tools that are designed to perform mechanical operations.
    b. Measuring tools are defined as tools that will measure work. Measuring tools can be classed as precision and non-precision tools.

2. Safety Precautions

    It is extremely important for all concerned to recognize the possibilities of injury when using handtools and measuring tools.
    The following safety precautions are included as a guide to prevent or minimize personal injury:

    a. Make certain all tool handles are securely attached before using them.
    b. Exercise extreme caution when handling edged tools.
    c. Do not use a tool for a purpose other than that for which it was intended.
    d. Do not handle tools carelessly carelessly piling tools in drawers, dropping tools on hard surfaces, etc., can damage tools. Damaged tools can cause mishaps.
    e. Keep your mind on your work so that you do not strike yourself or someone else with a hammer or sledge.
    f. Do not carry edged or pointed tools in your pocket.
    g. Always wear goggles when chipping metal and when grinding edges on tools.
    h. Hold driving tools correctly so that they will not slip off the work surface.
    i. Use the right tool for the job. The wrong tool may damage materials, injure workers, or both,
    j. Do not use punches with improper points or mushroomed heads,
    k. Do not use a tool that is oily or greasy. It may slip out of your hand, causing injury.
    l. When using jacks, make certain to use blocking or other supports when lifting a vehicle, in case of jack failure.
    m. Make sure work to be cut, sheared, chiseled, filed, etc., is steadied and secure, to prevent the tool from slipping.
    n. When using a knife, always cut away from your body, except in the case of a spoke shave or draw knife.
    o. Use torches and soldering irons with extreme care to prevent burns and explosions. The soldering iron must be so placed that the hot point cannot come in contact with flammable material or with the body.
    p. Familiarize yourself with the composition and hardness of the material to be worked.

II. MEASURING TOOLS
  1. General
      Measuring tools are designed for measuring work accurately. They include level indicating devices (levels), noncalibrated measuring tools (calipers, dividers, trammels) for transferring dimensions and/or layouts from one medium to another, calibrated measuring tools (rules, precision tapes, micrometers) designed to measure distances in accordance with one of several standards of measurement, gages (go and no-go gages, thread gages) which are machined to pre-determined shapes and/or sizes for measurement by comparison, and combination tools such as a combination square which is designed to perform two or more types of operation.

  2. Standards of Measurement
      a. Standards of Length
          Two systems, the English and Metric, are commonly used in the design of measuring tools for linear measurements. The English system uses inches, feet, and yards, while the Metric system uses millimeters, centimeters, and meters. In relation to each other, 1 inch is equivalent to 25.4 millimeters, or 1 millimeter is equivalent to 0.039370 inch.

      b. Standards of Screw Threads
          There are several screw thread systems that are recognized as standards throughout the world. All threaded items for Ordnance use in the United States, Great Britain, and Canada are specified in the Unified System. The existing inch-measure screw-thread systems should be understood despite the existence of the Unified System.

  (1) Inch-measure systems
  (a) Whitworth
          Introduced in England in 1941. The thread form is based on a 55 thread angle, and the crests and roots are rounded.
  (b) American National
          The American National screw-thread system was developed in 1933. This system is based on the 60 thread angle and the flat crests and roots and is included in the following series:
          1. Coarse thread sizes of 1 to 12 and 1/4 to 4".
          2. The fine thread series in sizes 0 to 12 and 1/4 to 1 1/2".
          3. The extra-fine thread series in sizes 0 to 12 and 1/2 to 2".
          4. The 8-pitch series in sizes from 1 to 6".
          5. The 12-pitch series from 1/2 to 6".
          6. The 16-pitch series from 3/4 to 4".
  (c) Classes of fit
      The American National screw-thread system calls for four regular classes of fit.
      Class   1. - Loose fit, with no possibility for interference between screw and tapped hole.

      2. - Medium or free fit, but permitting slight interference in the worst combination of maximum screw and maximum nut.

      3. - Close tolerances on mating parts may require this fit, applied to the highest grade of interchangeable work.

      4. - A fine snug fit, where a screwdriver or wrench may be necessary for assembly.

NOTE: An additional Class 5, or jaw fit, is recognized for studs.

(2) Unified system

Since the whitworth and American National thread forms do not assemble because of the difference in thread angle, the 60 thread angle was adapted in 1949; however, the British may still use rounded crests and roots and their products will assemble with those made in United States plants. In the Unified system, class signifies tolerance, or tolerance and allowance. It is determined by the selected combination of classes for mating external and internal threads. New classes of tolerance are listed below: 3 for screws, 1A, 2A, and 3A; and 3 for nuts, IB, 2B, and 3B.

(a) Classes 1A and 1B, loose fit

A fit giving quick and easy assembly, even when threads are bruised or dirty. Applications: Ordnance and special uses.

(b) Classes 2A and 2B, medium fit

This fit permits wrenching with minimum galling and seizure. This medium fit is suited for the majority of commercial fasteners and is interchangeable with the American National Class 2 fit.

(c) Classes 3A and 3B, close fit

No allowance is provided. Applications are those where close fit and accuracy of lead and thread angle are required.

c. Standards of Wire and Sheet Metal

Sheet metal, strip, wire, and tubing are produced with thickness diameters or wall thicknesses, according to several gaging systems, depending on the article and metal. This situation is the result of natural development and preferences of the industries that produce these products. No single standard for all manufacturers has been established, since practical considerations stand in the way of adoption. In the case of steel, large users are thoroughly familiar with the behavior of existing gages in tooling, especially dies, and do not intend that their shop personnel be burdened with learning how preferred thicknesses behave. Another important factor is the sum total of orders of warehouse stock manufactured with existing gages. You must keep abreast of any change in availability of metals in these common gaging systems, as opposed to simplified systems.

For example; in the brass industry, the American Standards Association (ASA) numbers are said to be preferred for simplicity of stocking, but actually most of the metal is still made to Brown and Sharpe (B&S) gage numbers.

(1) Sheet metal gaging systems

Several gaging systems are used for sheet and strip metal.

(a) Manufacturer's standard gaging system (Mfr's std)

This gaging system is currently used for carbon and alloy sheets. This system is based on steel weighing 41.82 psf, 1 inch thick. Gage thickness equivalents are based on 0.0014945 in. per oz. per sq. ft.; 0.023912 in. per lb. per sq. ft. (reciprocal of 41.82 lb. per sq. ft. per in. thick); 3.443329 in. per lb. per sq. in.

(b) U.S. standard gaging system (U.S. std)

This gaging system is obsolete except for stainless steel sheets, cold-rolled steel strip (both carbon and alloy), stainless steel tubing, and nickel-alloy sheet and strip.

(c) Birmingham wire gaging system (BWG)

This gaging system is also called the Stubs iron wire gaging system, and is used for hot-rolled steel carbon and alloy strip and steel tubing.

(d) Brown and Sharpe, or American wire gaging system (B&S or AWG)

This gaging system is used for copper strip, brass and bronze sheet and strip, and aluminum and wire magnesium sheet.

(2) Wire gaging systems

(a) Steel wire gaging system (SWG) or washburn & Moen gaging system

This gaging system is used for steel wire, carbon steel mechanical spring wire, alloy-steel spring wire, stainless steel wire, and so forth. Carbon steel or music wire (wire used in the manufacture of musical instruments) is nominally specified to the sizes in the American Steel & Wire Company music wire sizes, although it is referred to by a number of other names found in steel catalogs.

(b) Brown & Sharpe (B&S) or American wire gaging system (AWG)

This gaging system is used for copper, copper alloy, aluminum, magnesium, nickel alloy, and other nonferrous metal wires used commercially.

(3) Rod gaging systems

The Brown & Sharpe gaging system is used for copper, brass, and aluminum rods. Steel rods are nominally listed in fractional sizes, but drill rod may be listed in stubs steel wire gage or the twist drill and steel wire gage. It is preferable to refer to twist drill sizes in inch equivalents instead of the Stubs or twist drill numbers.

d. Standards of Weight

Two standards of weight that are most commonly used are the Metric and English weight measures.

(1) Metric standards

The principal unit of weight in the Metric system is the gram (gm). Multiples of grams are obtained by prefixing the Greek words deka (10), hekto (100), and kilo (1,000). Divisions are obtained by prefixing the Latin words deci (1/10), centi (1/100), and milli (1/1000). The gram is the weight of 1 cubic centimeter of puje distilled water at a temperature of 39.2° F.; the kilogram is the weight of 1 liter (one cubic decimeter) of pureQdistilled water at a temperature of 39.2° F.; the metric ton is the weight of 1 cubic meter of pyre distilled water at a temperature of 39.2° F.

(2) English standards

The principal unit of weight in the English system is the grain (gr). We are more familiar with the ounce (oz), which is equal to 437.5 grains.

3. Useful Measuring Tools
   a. Levels
      (1) Purpose

Levels are tools designed to prove whether a plane or surface is true horizontal or true vertical. Some levels are calibrated so that they will indicate the angle inclination in relation to a horizontal or vertical surface in degrees, minutes, and seconds.

   b. Plumb Bobs
      (1) Purpose

The common plumb bob is used to determine true verticality. It is used in carpentry when erecting vertical uprights and corner posts of framework. Surveyors use it for transferring and lining up points. Special plumb bobs are designed for use with steel tapes or line to measure tank contents (oil, water, etc.).

   c. Scribers
      (1) Purpose

Scribers are used to mark and lay out a pattern of work, to be followed in subsequent machining operations. Scribers are made for scribing, scoring, or marking many different materials such as glass, steel, aluminium, copper, and so forth.

   d. Rules or Scales
      (1) Purpose

All rules (scales) are used to measure linear dimensions. They are read by a comparison of the etched lines on the scale with an edge or surface. Most scale dimensions are read with the naked eye, although a magnifying glass can be used to read graduations on a scale smaller than 1/64 inch.

   e. Precision Tapes
      (1) Purpose

Precision tapes are used for measuring circumferences and long distances where rules cannot be applied.

   f. Squares
      (1) Purpose

The purpose of a square is to test work for squareness and trueness. It is also used as a guide when marking work for subsequent machining, sawing, planing, and chiseling operations.

   g. Calipers and Dividers

(1) Purpose

Dividers are used for measuring distances between two points, for transferring or comparing measurements directly from a rule, or for scribing an arc, radius, or circle. Calipers are used for measuring diameters and distances, or for comparing dimensions or sizes with standards such as a graduated rule,

h. Micrometers

(1) Purpose

Micrometers are used for measurements requiring precise accuracy. They are more reliable and more accurate than the calipers listed in the preceding section.

i. Surface, Depth, and Height Gages

(1) Purpose

(a) Surface Gage

A surface gage is a measuring tool generally used to transfer measurements to work by scribing a line, and to indicate the accuracy or parallelism of surfaces.

(b) Depth Gage

A depth gage is an instrument adapted to measuring the depth of holes, slots, counterborers, recesses, and the distance from a surface to some recessed part.

(c) Height Gage

A height gage is used in the layout of jigs and fixtures, and on a bench, where it is used to check the location of holes and surfaces. It accurately measures and marks off vertical distances from a plane surface.

(d) Surface Plate

A surface plate provides a true, smooth, plane surface. It is often used in conjunction with surface and height gages as a level base on which the gages and parts are placed to obtain accurate measurements,

j. Plug, Ring, and Snap Gages and Gage Blocks

(1) Purpose

Plug, ring, and snap gages, and precision gage blocks are used as standards to determine whether or not one or more dimensions of a manufactured part are within specified limits. Their measurements are included in the construction of each gage, and they are called fixed gages; however, some snap gages are adjustable. In the average shop, gages are used for a wide range of work, from rough machining to the finest tool and die making. The accuracy required of the same type gage will be different, depending on the application. The following classes of gages and their limits of accuracy are standard for all makes:

Class XX(Male gages only).

Precision lapped to laboratory tolerances. For master or setup standards.

Class X

Precision lapped to close tolerances for many types of masters and the highest quality working and inspection gages.
Class Y
Good lapped finish to slightly increased tolerances for inspection and working gages.

Class Z
Commercial finish (ground and polished, but not fully lapped) for a large percentage of working gages in which tolerances are fairly wide, and where production quantities are not so large.

Class ZZ(Ring gages only)
Ground only to meet the demand for an inexpensive gage, where quantities are small and tolerances liberal.

k. Miscellaneous Measuring Gages
(1) Purpose
    (a) Thickness (Feeler) Gages
        These gages are fixed in leaf form, which permits the checking and measuring of small openings such as contact points, narrow slots, and so forth. They are widely used to check the flatness of parts in straightening and grinding operations and in squaring objects with a try square.
    (b) Wire and Drill Gages
        The wire gage is used for gaging metal wire, and a similar gage is also used to check the size of hot and cold rolled steel, sheet and plate iron, and music wire. Drill gages determine the size of a drill and indicate the correct size of drill to use for given tap size. Drill number and decimal size are also shown in this type gage.
    (c) Drill Rods or Blanks
        Drill rods or blanks are used on line inspection work to check the size of drilled holes in the same manner as with plug gages. They are also used for setup inspection to check the location of holes.
    (d) Thread Gages
        Among the many gages used in connection with the machining and inspection of threads are the center gage and the screw pitch gages.
        1. Center gage
            The center gage is used to set thread cutting tools. Four scales on the gage are used for determining the number of threads per inch.
        2. Screw pitch gage
            Screw pitch gages are used to determine the pitch of an unknown thread. The pitch of a screw thread is the distance between the center of one tooth to the center of the next tooth.
    (e) Small Hole Gage Set
        This set of 4 or more gages is used to check dimensions of small holes, slots, groves etc., from approximately 1/8 to 1/2" in diameter.

    (f)   Telescoping Gages

These gages are used for measuring the inside size of slots or holes up to 6" in width or diameter.

    (g)   Thread Cutting Tool Gages

These gages provide a standard for thread cutting tools. They have an enclosed angle of 29 and include a 29 setting tool. One gage furnishes the correct form for square threads and the other for Acme standard threads.

    (h)   Fillet and Radius Gages

These gages are used to check convex and concave radii in corners or against shoulders.

    (i)   Drill Point Gage

This gage is used to check the accuracy of drill cutting edges after grinding. It is also equipped with a 6" hook rule. This tool can be used as a drill point gage, hook rule, plain rule, and a slide caliper for taking outside measurements.

    (j)   Marking Gages

A marking gage is used to mark off guidelines parallel to an edge, end, or surface of a piece of wood. It has a sharp spur or pin that does the marking.

    (k)   Tension Gage

This type of gage is used to check contact point pressure and brush spring tension in 1 ounce graduations.

    (l)   Saw Tooth Micrometer Gage

This special gage checks the depth of saw teeth in thousandths of an inch from 0 to 0.075 inch.

III.   NONEDGED TOOLS

    1.   General

This title encompasses a large group of general purpose hand-tools. These tools are termed nonedged hand-tools because they are not used for cutting purposes and do not have sharpened or cutting edges. They are designed to facilitate mechanical operations such as clamping, hammering, twisting, turning, etc. This group includes such tools as hammers, mallets, and screwdrivers; which are commonly referred to as driving tools. Other types of nonedged tools are wrenches, pliers, clamps, pullers, soldering irons, torches, and many others of similar nature. Several types of pliers have cutting edges (exceptions to the rule).

    2.   Useful Nonedged Tools

        a.   Hammers and Mallets

           (1) Purpose

Hammers and mallets are used to drive nails, spikes, drift pins, bolts, and wedges. They are also used to strike chisels, punches, and to shape metals. Sledge hammers are used to drive spikes and large nails, to break rock and concrete, and to drift heavy timbers.

        b.   Screwdrivers

           (1) Purpose

Screwdrivers are used for driving or removing screws or bolts with slotted or special heads.

c. Wrenches
   (1)   Purpose

Wrenches are used to tighten or loosen nuts, bolts, screws, and pipe plugs. Special wrenches are made to grip round stock, such as pipe, studs, and rods. Spanner wrenches are used to turn cover plates, rings and couplings.

d. Pliers and Tongs
   (1)   Purpose

Pliers are used for gripping, cutting, bending, forming, or holding work, and for special jobs. Tongs look like long-handled pliers and are mainly used for holding or handling hot pieces of metal work to be forged or quenched, or hot pieces of glass.

e. Clamping Devices
   (1)   Purpose

Vises are used for holding work on the bench when it is being planed, sawed, drilled, shaped, sharpened, riveted, or when wood is being glued. Clamps are used for holding work that cannot be satisfactorily held in a vise because of its shape or size, or when a vise is not available. Clamps are generally used for light work.

f. Jacks
   (1)   Purpose

Jacks are used to raise or lower work and heavy loads short distances. Some jacks are used for pushing and pulling operations, or for spreading and clamping.

g. Bars and Mattock
   (1)   Purpose

Bars are heavy steel tools used to lift and move heavy objects and to pry where leverage is needed. They are also used to remove nails and spikes during wrecking operations. The mattock is used for digging in hard ground, cutting Toots irnderground, und to loosen clay formations in which there is little or no rock. The mattock may also be used for light prying when no bars are available,

h. Soldering Irons
   (1)   Purpose

Soldering is joining two pieces of metal by adhesion. The soldering iron is the source of heat by melting solder and heating the parts to be joined to the proper temperature.

i. Grinders and Sharpening Stones
   (1)   Purpose

Grinders are devices that are designed to mount abrasive wheels that will wear away other materials to varying degrees. Special grinders are designed to receive engine valves. Sharpening stones are used for whetting or final sharpening of sharp edged tools that have been ground to shape or to a fine point on a grinder,

j. Benders and Pullers
   (1)   Purpose

Benders are designed to facilitate bending brass or copper pipe and tubing.Pullers are designed to facilitate pulling operations such as removing bearings, gears, wheels, pulleys, sheaves, bushings, cylinder sleeves, shafts, and other close-fitting parts.

k. Torches

(1) Purpose

Torches are used as sources of heat in soldering, sweating, tinning, burning, and other miscellaneous jobs where heat is required.

l. Blacksmith's Anvils and Iron Working Tools

(1) Purpose

Blacksmith's anvils are designed to provide a working surface when punching holes through metal and for supporting the metal when it is being forged and shaped. Iron working tools such as flatters, fullers, swages, hardies, and set hammers are used to form or shape forgings. Heading tools are used to shape bolts.

m. Breast Drill and Ratchet Bit Brace

(1) Purpose

The breast drill and ratchet bit brace are used to hold various kinds of bits and twist drills used in boring and reaming holes and to drive screws, nuts, and bolts.

n. Sheet Metal Tools

(1) Purpose

Sheet metal working tools consist of stakes, dolly blocks, calking tools, rivet sets, and dolly bars. Punches, shears, and hammers are also sheet metal working tools. However, they are covered in other sections of this text. Rivet sets and dolly bars are used to form heads on rivets after joining sections of sheet metal and steel work. Stakes are used to support sheet metal while the metal is being shaped. Calking tools are used to shape joints of sheet metal. Dolly blocks are used conjunction with bumping body hammers to straighten out damaged sheet metal.

IV. EDGED HANDTOOLS

1. General

Edged handtools are designed with sharp edges for working on metal, wood, plastic, leather, cloth, glass, and other materials. They are used to remove portions from the work or to separate the work into sections by cutting, punching, scraping, chiseling, filing, and so forth.

2. Useful Edged Eandtools

a. Chisels

(1) Purpose

Chisels are made to cut wood, metal hard putty, and other materials. Woodworker's chisels are used to pare off and cut wood. Cold chisels are used to chip and cut cold metal. Some blacksmith's chisels are used to cut hot metal. A special chisel that is available is used to cut hard putty so that glass may be removed from its frame channel.

b. Files

(1) Purpose

Files are used for cutting, smoothing off, or removing small amounts of metal.

c. Knives

(1) Purpose

Most knives are used to cut, pare, notch, and trim wood, leather, rubber, and other materials. Some knives used by glaziers are called putty knives; these are used to apply and spread putty when installing glass.

d. Scrapers

(1) Purpose

Some scrapers are used for trueing metal, wood, and plastic surfaces which have previously been machined or filed. Other scrapers are made to remove paint, stencil markings, and other coatings from various surfaces.

e. Punches

(1) Purpose

Punches are used to punch holes in metal, leather, paper, and other materials; mark metal, drive pins or rivets; to free frozen pins from their holes; and aline holes in different sections of metal. Special punches are designed to install grommets and snap fasteners. Bench mounted punching machines are used to punch holes in metal one at a time, or up to 12 holes simultaneously.

f. Awls

(1) Purpose

A saddler's awl is used for forcing holes in cloth or leather to make sewing easier. A scratch awl is used for making a center point or a small hole and for scribing lines on wood and plastics.

g. Shears, Nippers, and Pincers

(1) Purpose

Shears are used for cutting sheet metal and steel of various thicknesses and shapes. Nippers are used to cut metal off flush with a surface, and likewise to cut wire, light metal bars, bolts, and nails. Pincers are used to pull out nails, bolts, and pins.

h. Bolt, Cable, and Glass Cutters

(1) Purpose

Cutters or clippers are used to cut bolts, rods, wire rope, cable, screws, rivets, nuts, bars, strips, and wire. Special cutters are made to cut glass.

i. Piper and Tube Cutters, and Flaring Tools

(1) Purpose

Pipe cutters are used to cut pipe made of steel, brass, copper, wrought iron, and lead. Tube cutters are used to cut tube made of iron, steel, brass, copper, and aluminum. The essential difference is that tubing has considerably thinner walls are compared to pipe. Flaring tools are used to make single or double flares in the ends of tubing,

j. Reamers

(1) Purpose

Reamers are used to smoothly enlarge drilled holes to an exact size and to finish the hole at the same time. Reamers are also used to remove burrs from the inside diameters of pipe and drilled holes,

k. Taps and Dies

    (1) Purpose

        Taps and dies are used to cut threads in metal, plastics, or hard rubber. The taps are used for cutting internal threads, and the dies are used to cut external threads.

l. Thread Chasers

    (1) Purpose

        Thread chasers are used to re-thread damaged external or internal threads,

m. Screw and Tap Extractors

    (1) Purpose

        Screw extractors are used to remove broken screws without damaging the surrounding material or the threaded hole. Tap extractors are used to remove broken taps.

ANSWER SHEET

PART_____ TITLE OF POSITION_____

(AS GIVEN IN EXAMINATION ANNOUNCEMENT - INCLUDE OPTION, IF ANY)

F EXAMINATION _____

(CITY OR TOWN)   (STATE)   DATE_____

RATING

USE THE SPECIAL PENCIL.   MAKE GLOSSY BLACK MARKS.

Make only ONE mark for each answer.   Additional and stray marks may be counted as mistakes.   In making corrections, erase errors COMPLETELY.

ANSWER SHEET

TEST NO. _____ PART _____ TITLE OF POSITION _____

(AS GIVEN IN EXAMINATION ANNOUNCEMENT - INCLUDE OPTION, IF ANY)

PLACE OF EXAMINATION _____ DATE _____

(CITY OR TOWN)   (STATE)

RATING

USE THE SPECIAL PENCIL.   MAKE GLOSSY BLACK MARKS.

	A	B	C	D	E		A	B	C	D	E		A	B	C	D	E		A	B	C	D	E		A	B	C	D	E
1						26						51						76						101					
2						27						52						77						102					
3						28						53						78						103					
4						29						54						79						104					
5						30						55						80						105					
6						31						56						81						106					
7						32						57						82						107					
8						33						58						83						108					
9						34						59						84						109					
10						35						60						85						110					

Make only ONE mark for each answer.   Additional and stray marks may be
counted as mistakes.   In making corrections, erase errors COMPLETELY.

	A	B	C	D	E		A	B	C	D	E		A	B	C	D	E		A	B	C	D	E		A	B	C	D	E
11						36						61						86						111					
12						37						62						87						112					
13						38						63						88						113					
14						39						64						89						114					
15						40						65						90						115					
16						41						66						91						116					
17						42						67						92						117					
18						43						68						93						118					
19						44						69						94						119					
20						45						70						95						120					
21						46						71						96						121					
22						47						72						97						122					
23						48						73						98						123					
24						49						74						99						124					
25						50						75						100						125					